Issues
Annual Index
2004

ISSUES

Compiled by
Isobel McLean

Independence

Educational Publishers
Cambridge

First published by Independence
PO Box 295
Cambridge CB1 3XP

ISBN 1 86168 299 9

Printed in Great Britain
MWL Print Group Ltd

Typeset by
Claire Boyd

A

abattoirs **19.**25, 26, 28

abortion

after-effects

emotional **71.**8, 27, 31-2

longer term **71.**27

and mental health **71.**27, 30, 31-2, 34-6

physical **71.**2, 26-7

age of women having **71.**5

arguments against (pro-life) **71.**2, 16, 20, 24-5

and backstreet abortions **71.**20-1

and disabled babies **71.**21, 24

and rape **71.**21, 24

and saving the life of the mother **71.**21, 24

and very young mothers **71.**24

arguments for (pro-choice) **71.**2, 20

and bereavement **71.**25

and breast cancer **71.**16, 36

case studies **71.**30-3

and consent of partners **71.**22

deaths from **20.**25, 27, 30; **71.**16

decision-making **71.**6-7

early abortion

costs **71.**1

methods **71.**1-2, 13

and emergency contraception (the morning-after pill) **71.**6, 11, 12, 22-3

and under 16s **71.**28-9

and euthanasia **4.**3, 31

feminist case for **71.**18

and fetal abnormality **71.**5

and genetic research **71.**17

having sex after **71.**27

and humanism **71.**3, 15, 17-18

illegal (backstreet) abortions **71.**16, 20-1

Irish abortion **71.**5, 8, 16

late abortion **71.**8, 18

methods **71.**2, 7

reasons for **71.**4-5

and Scottish women **71.**38

law **71.**1, 7, 12-13, 18-19, 36-7

and married women **71.**5, 37

and men

abortions instigated by **71.**36

information for **71.**26-7

rights of fathers **71.**25

and mental health **71.**34-6

methods

and conscious sedation **71.**23

and local anaesthetic **71.**23, 33

medical abortion ('the abortion pill') **71.**1-2, 7, 10, 13, 22, 23

vacuum aspiration ('the suction method') **71.**2, 7

and the NHS

case studies **71.**32, 33

funding **71.**4, 29-30

obtaining an abortion **71.**1

problems facing women **71.**29-30

and Northern Ireland **71.**7, 8, 19, 29, 36

organisations **71.**37

post-abortion counselling **71.**27, 31, 34

post-abortion syndrome (PAS) **71.**16

post-abortion trauma **71.**33, 35

premature deliveries **71.**21

private abortions **71.**1, 38

public opinion on **71.**2-3, 16, 30

questions and answers on **71.**8, 12-13, 22-5

and rape **71.**3, 18, 21, 24

religious positions on **71.**3, 8, 14-16, 17, 36

safety of **71.**6, 8

and sex selection of the foetus **71.**17, 18

and sexual health **10.**1, 37

statistics **71.**4-5, 36

and suicide **71.**35, 36

talking about **71.**37

and teenage pregnancies **20.**30, 34; **67.**3, 4; **70.**11; **71.**5, 8, 9-11, 28-9; **75.**1, 3, 4, 17

under 16s **71.**1, 10-12, 19, 28-9, 36, 37, 39

and women from abroad **71.**5

absent fathers, relationships with children **75.**36

absenteeism

costs of **25.**5, 14

Volume numbers appear first (in bold) followed by page numbers; a change in volume number is preceded by a semi-colon.

Vol. 3 The Animal Rights Debate

Vol. 4 The Euthanasia Issue

Vol. 10 Sexually Transmitted Diseases

Vol. 11 Fertility Rights

Vol. 16 Our Ageing World

Vol. 19 Looking at Vegetarianism

Vol. 20 Population Growth

Vol. 22 Confronting Child Abuse

Vol. 23 Sexuality

Vol. 25 The Changing Workplace

Vol. 27 The Censorship Issue

Vol. 28 The Global Warming Debate

Vol. 29 Gambling

Vol. 31 The Impact of the Internet

Vol. 32 Coping with Stress

Vol. 33 The Tourism Issue

Vol. 35 The Education Crisis?

Vol. 39 Alcohol Abuse

Vol. 40 The Future of Marriage

Vol. 43 A Consumer Society

Vol. 44 Confronting Domestic Violence

Vol. 46 Child Labour

Vol. 54 The Energy Debate

Vol. 55 Globalisation

Vol. 56 The Wealth Divide

Vol. 57 Waste Pollution

Vol. 58 The Transport Issue

Vol. 59 Issues in Sport

Vol. 60 Confronting Cancer

Vol. 61 Fitness

Vol. 62 Drugs and the Law

Vol. 63 The Racism Debate

Vol. 64 The Gender Issue

Vol. 65 Human Rights

Vol. 66 Self-Esteem

Vol. 67 Parenting

Vol. 68 Coping with Depression

Vol. 69 The Media

Vol. 70 Adolescent Health

Vol. 71 Abortion

Vol. 72 Obesity and Eating Disorders

Vol. 73 Dealing with Bullies

Vol. 74 Money Matters

Vol. 75 Lone-Parent Families

Vol. 76 The Water Crisis

Vol. 77 Self-inflicted Violence

Vol. 78 Threatened Species

Vol. 79 Dealing with Homelessness

Vol. 80 The Cannabis Debate

Vol. 81 Alternative Therapies

Vol. 82 Protecting our Privacy

Vol. 83 Dealing with Crime

Vol. 84 Mental Wellbeing

Vol. 85 The Housing Crisis

Vol. 86 Smoking and your Health

Vol. 87 Genetic Modification

Vol. 88 Food and Nutrition

Vol. 89 Refugees

Vol. 90 Human and Animal Cloning

Vol. 91 Disability Issues

and excessive drinking **39.**21
and work-related stress **32.**20-1, 26, 27, 28, 29
abstinence education **75.**18, 26-7
abusive relationships
    defining **44.**1
    and low self-esteem **66.**6, 10, 12
    reasons for staying in **44.**1, 4, 34
    and self-harm **77.**10, 14
    and witnessing domestic violence as a child **44.**12-13
    and young runaways **79.**25, 29
academic achievement *see* educational achievement
access audits **91.**10-11, 14, 15-16
accidents
    accidental death of children **56.**2
    alcohol as a contributory factor in **39.**21, 27
    see also road accidents
acetone **86.**4
acid rain **28.**4, 11; **54.**5, 7, 54; **76.**11
acne, and milk consumption **19.**18
acupressure **81.**1, 3
acupuncture **81.**5-6, 14, 23, 36; **86.**30, 37
adolescent health
    and confidentiality **70.**6
    and diabetes **70.**3, 27, 28
    and drug abuse **70.**6, 7, 8, 14-16
    in the European Union **70.**8-9
    general health and wellbeing **70.**1-3
    health needs **70.**3-4, 6-8
    and illness **70.**6
    and nutrition **70.**6
    and obesity **70.**4, 9, 27, 28, 29-30
    psychosomatic symptoms **70.**8
    and self-report **70.**1
adoption
    and birth parents, tracing **11.**36, 37-8
    and children's rights **65.**1-2, 3
    by gay people **23.**38
    and pregnancies as a result of rape **71.**24
    statistics **40.**1
    and surrogacy **11.**21, 25
    and teenage pregnancies **71.**10
    tracing birth parents **11.**36, 37-8

and unwanted pregnancies **71.**12, 18
advance directives *see* living wills
advertising **69.**11-15, 28-30
    age limits in job adverts **16.**13
    agencies and the Communications Bill **69.**20
    alcohol **39.**3, 6, 7, 13, 14
    British meat **19.**4, 40
    and children **43.**6, 7, 8, 9; **69.**11-13, 14
    cigarettes **86.**5, 8, 26
    cigarettes and tobacco **70.**7-8, 18
    cinema **69.**30
    direct mail **69.**29
    junk food **72.**11, 14; **88.**10, 11, 19, 20, 35, 37
    leaflet distribution **69.**29
    in magazines **69.**14, 28-9
    in newspapers **69.**28-9
    outdoor **69.**29
    point of sale (POS) **69.**29-30
    radio **69.**21, 28
    safe sex campaign **10.**3, 11
    television **69.**3, 12, 26, 29
    use of swearing in **27.**39
affirmative action **63.**4
affordable housing **85.**29-31
    and the exception site policy **85.**28
    giving public money to private developers **85.**19
    and homelessness **79.**1, 2, 9, 11-12, 35
    and housing associations **85.**19
    large houses **85.**11
    policies **85.**28-30
    and public sector workers **85.**1, 3, 4, 20, 21, 22
    in rural areas **85.**5, 28, 31
    shortage of **85.**1, 3, 8-9, 20
    and social housing **85.**8
    and young workers **85.**3-4
age
    and abortion **71.**5
    and attitudes to advertising **69.**14
    and attitudes to illegal drugs **80.**27-8
    and body-fat levels **61.**14-15
    and breast cancer **60.**23
    consent for gay sex **23.**17, 19, 29-30, 39, 40

Volume numbers appear first (in bold) followed by page numbers; a change in volume number is preceded by a semi-colon.

Vol. 3   The Animal Rights Debate
Vol. 4   The Euthanasia Issue
Vol. 10 Sexually Transmitted Diseases
Vol. 11 Fertility Rights
Vol. 16 Our Ageing World
Vol. 19 Looking at Vegetarianism
Vol. 20 Population Growth
Vol. 22 Confronting Child Abuse
Vol. 23 Sexuality
Vol. 25 The Changing Workplace
Vol. 27 The Censorship Issue
Vol. 28 The Global Warming Debate
Vol. 29 Gambling
Vol. 31 The Impact of the Internet
Vol. 32 Coping with Stress
Vol. 33 The Tourism Issue
Vol. 35 The Education Crisis?
Vol. 39 Alcohol Abuse
Vol. 40 The Future of Marriage
Vol. 43 A Consumer Society

Vol. 44 Confronting Domestic Violence
Vol. 46 Child Labour
Vol. 54 The Energy Debate
Vol. 55 Globalisation
Vol. 56 The Wealth Divide
Vol. 57 Waste Pollution
Vol. 58 The Transport Issue
Vol. 59 Issues in Sport
Vol. 60 Confronting Cancer
Vol. 61 Fitness
Vol. 62 Drugs and the Law
Vol. 63 The Racism Debate
Vol. 64 The Gender Issue
Vol. 65 Human Rights
Vol. 66 Self-Esteem
Vol. 67 Parenting
Vol. 68 Coping with Depression
Vol. 69 The Media
Vol. 70 Adolescent Health
Vol. 71 Abortion

Vol. 72 Obesity and Eating Disorders
Vol. 73 Dealing with Bullies
Vol. 74 Money Matters
Vol. 75 Lone-Parent Families
Vol. 76 The Water Crisis
Vol. 77 Self-inflicted Violence
Vol. 78 Threatened Species
Vol. 79 Dealing with Homelessness
Vol. 80 The Cannabis Debate
Vol. 81 Alternative Therapies
Vol. 82 Protecting our Privacy
Vol. 83 Dealing with Crime
Vol. 84 Mental Wellbeing
Vol. 85 The Housing Crisis
Vol. 86 Smoking and your Health
Vol. 87 Genetic Modification
Vol. 88 Food and Nutrition
Vol. 89 Refugees
Vol. 90 Human and Animal Cloning
Vol. 91 Disability Issues

and contraception **75**.15
of criminal responsibility **83**.29-30
and dementia **84**.11, 12
and depressive illness **68**.1, 9
and drug misuse
   and mental illness **62**.8
   in the UK **62**.4-5, 20
and ethnic minorities in the UK **63**.6
and fertility **67**.33
and first-time house buyers **85**.7
and food, eating disorders **70**.35
and gambling **29**.2, 8, 27, 34-5, 35-6
and Internet access **31**.1; **69**.3
of lone parents **75**.28
of marriage **40**.1, 3, 5-7, 13-14, 20
of missing persons **79**.13
of motherhood **67**.3, 4, 6, 18
of self-harmers **77**.6
of smokers **86**.1
and suicide rates **77**.2, 17
and television viewing **69**.2, 4
of young offenders **83**.15
age discrimination
   in employment **16**.3, 11, 13-27
   in health care **16**.11, 28, 35
   and unemployment **16**.16, 17, 20, 25
ageing population **20**.4, 5, 9, 33; **43**.3; **75**.29
   attitudes to the **16**.24
   definitions of 'old age' **16**.5
   in developing countries **20**.9, 11
   and health **16**.5, 28-40
   increase in **16**.4
   myths and misconceptions **16**.5-6
   old-age dependency ratio **16**.4
   oldest old **16**.1, 4
   and pensions **16**.25-7
   and replacement migration **20**.15, 16
   services for the **20**.34-5
   stereotypes about older people **16**.3
   in the UK **16**.1-3, 8-11
   in urban areas **16**.4
   world-wide **16**.4, 7, 10
aggressive behaviour
   avoiding **66**.28
   and children's self-esteem **66**.29
agoraphobia **84**.16
agricultural experiments on animals **3**.8
agricultural land
   degradation of **20**.3, 8, 9, 13, 14, 23, 24
   and new house-building **85**.28, 33
   and population growth **20**.1, 8
agriculture
   and child labour **65**.17
   and climate change **28**.10, 14, 16
   crops for green energy **54**.12, 18, 26, 27
   employment of children in **46**.2-3
   farming productivity **87**.15, 23-4
   and food nutrition **88**.31-4
   free trade in agriculture **88**.33
   and global trade rules **55**.40
   and global water shortages **76**.3, 4, 8
   and globalisation **55**.1-2
   and Globally Threatened Birds **78**.8
   and methane emissions **28**.8, 11
   productivity **87**.15, 23-4
   subsidies **55**.33; **56**.36, 37
   and water management **76**.18
   and water pollution **76**.11
   water use by **76**.36
AIDS (Acquired Immune Deficiency Syndrome) **10**.14
   and adolescents **70**.1, 9
   and animal research **3**.15, 17
   and child marriages **65**.19
   and child prostitution **46**.20, 21, 22, 26
   children with **10**.14, 16
   and children's rights **65**.15, 16, 23
   and complementary medicine **81**.39
   deaths due to **10**.1, 14-17, 21, 26-7, 33, 35
   and dementia **16**.37
   in developing countries **10**.16, 26-7; **20**.20, 34; **55**.38
   and development aid **56**.35
   diagnosis of **10**.20
   global crisis **10**.14
   and homosexuality **10**.2, 14, 20, 21; **23**.12, 17, 24
   numbers of people with in the UK **10**.20
   and older people **16**.7
   and population growth **20**.3, 5, 7, 11
   prevention programmes **20**.25, 27, 28, 30, 37
   public attitudes to **10**.14-15, 20
   and sex education **75**.21, 22
   and sexual behaviour **75**.16
   statistics **20**.36
   worldwide epidemic statistics **10**.16-17
   see also HIV (human immunodeficiency virus)
air pollution
   and air transport **58**.17-18
   and global warming **28**.3, 13, 23-4, 25-7, 39
   and traffic **58**.1, 5, 8, 9-10, 15
air travel **33**.4
alcohol **88**.7, 24
   advertising **39**.3, 6, 7, 13, 14
   alcohol-related deaths **39**.1, 5, 6, 9, 11, 15, 18, 24
      numbers of **39**.34
   and body weight **61**.17, 31
   and cancer **39**.37; **60**.1, 15
   and cannabis **62**.27; **80**.8-9, 21
   consumption
      and ethnic minorities **63**.7; **67**.6
      guidelines **39**.8-9, 25-6, 35-6
      and obesity **72**.2
      in the UK **39**.6, 24, 40
      wine and spirits **43**.2
      see also young people and alcohol
   deaths caused by **80**.10
   dependence syndrome **39**.15
   as a depressant drug **39**.1, 9, 10, 15
   and depression **68**.4, 19
   drink-driving **39**.3, 10, 18, 26, 35
   and drug misuse **62**.1, 7-8, 15
   effects of **39**.1, 8, 15
   and footballers **59**.39
   hangovers **39**.2, 10, 36

health benefits **39.**7, 9, 26, 37
health risks **39.**2, 5, 10, 15, 16, 25-8, 35
industry **39.**3, 40
and mental illness **84.**3, 27
   schizophrenia **84.**14
myths about **39.**2
and other drugs **80.**26
red wine **39.**37
social and controlled drinking patterns **39.**9
strength of in drinks **39.**1, 6
and stress **32.**28, 33, 34, 35, 39
testing your knowledge about **39.**34
tolerance to **39.**15, 36
and the UK law **39.**4
units of **39.**1-2, 9, 15, 28
alcohol abuse **39.**9, 14, 28-40
   binge-drinking **39.**6, 8, 14, 18, 20, 21, 25; **70.**20-4
   blackouts **39.**40
   causes of alcoholism **39.**15-16
   characteristics of alcoholism **39.**16
   and children and young people in prison **83.**23
   coping with parents who drink too much **39.**14, 30-2
   counselling for **39.**37
   cutting down on underage drinking **83.**35-6
   defining **39.**32, 35, 37-8, 39-40
   and depression **39.**16
   dishonesty of **39.**22-3
   and domestic violence **44.**4-5
   help for **39.**33, 36, 37-8
   and homelessness **79.**2, 7, 10, 15, 16
   and mental health problems **39.**28
   and missing persons **79.**13
   numbers of alcoholics **39.**15
   and prisoners on remand **83.**26
   reasons for **39.**23
   and self-esteem **66.**6, 20
   and self-harm **77.**10, 13, 24
   and suicide **77.**3, 4, 23
   symptoms **39.**16, 35
   and teenage sex **75.**18
   treatment of alcoholism **39.**16-17
      changing habits **39.**29

   detoxification **39.**17, 36-7
   family therapy **39.**17
   rehabilitative treatment therapy **39.**17
   relapse prevention **39.**17
   self-help groups **39.**17, 29, 38
   withdrawal symptoms **39.**36-7
in the workplace **39.**21-2
and yob-culture Britain **83.**5
and young offenders **83.**15
allergenicity of GM crops **87.**8, 17, 18, 19-20
alternative medicine *see* complementary medicine (CM)
aluminium recycling **57.**2, 4, 22-3, 27, 30
ammonia **86.**4, 10
amniocentesis tests **71.**21
amphetamines **62.**2
   adulterated **62.**13
   and the law **62.**21
   and patterns of drug use **62.**4, 14
   quantity seized in the UK **62.**3
amphibians
   and evolution **78.**1
   and the exotic pet trade **78.**21
   natterjack toads **78.**29
amputations **86.**10
amyl nitrate **62.**4, 21
anabolic agents/steroids **59.**20, 23-4, 29; **62.**4, 14, 21-2
anaemia, and iron deficiency **19.**5
anaesthetics, and animal experiments **3.**16
anger management, and self-esteem **66.**3, 5
animal cloning **90.**2, 15, 26-39
   and animal welfare **90.**35
   birth defects **90.**27, 28, 31, 34, 35, 39
   birth weight problems **90.**27-8, 35
   endangered species **90.**21, 30
   ethics of **90.**29-30, 33
   farm animals **90.**30, 39
   for food **90.**39
   health of cloned animals **90.**27, 28, 31, 34, 39
   history of **90.**27
   Kaguya the mouse **90.**36
   medical value to people **90.**34
   mice **90.**36

Volume numbers appear first (in bold) followed by page numbers; a change in volume number is preceded by a semi-colon.

Vol. **3** The Animal Rights Debate
Vol. **4** The Euthanasia Issue
Vol. **10** Sexually Transmitted Diseases
Vol. **11** Fertility Rights
Vol. **16** Our Ageing World
Vol. **19** Looking at Vegetarianism
Vol. **20** Population Growth
Vol. **22** Confronting Child Abuse
Vol. **23** Sexuality
Vol. **25** The Changing Workplace
Vol. **27** The Censorship Issue
Vol. **28** The Global Warming Debate
Vol. **29** Gambling
Vol. **31** The Impact of the Internet
Vol. **32** Coping with Stress
Vol. **33** The Tourism Issue
Vol. **35** The Education Crisis?
Vol. **39** Alcohol Abuse
Vol. **40** The Future of Marriage
Vol. **43** A Consumer Society

Vol. **44** Confronting Domestic Violence
Vol. **46** Child Labour
Vol. **54** The Energy Debate
Vol. **55** Globalisation
Vol. **56** The Wealth Divide
Vol. **57** Waste Pollution
Vol. **58** The Transport Issue
Vol. **59** Issues in Sport
Vol. **60** Confronting Cancer
Vol. **61** Fitness
Vol. **62** Drugs and the Law
Vol. **63** The Racism Debate
Vol. **64** The Gender Issue
Vol. **65** Human Rights
Vol. **66** Self-Esteem
Vol. **67** Parenting
Vol. **68** Coping with Depression
Vol. **69** The Media
Vol. **70** Adolescent Health
Vol. **71** Abortion

Vol. **72** Obesity and Eating Disorders
Vol. **73** Dealing with Bullies
Vol. **74** Money Matters
Vol. **75** Lone-Parent Families
Vol. **76** The Water Crisis
Vol. **77** Self-inflicted Violence
Vol. **78** Threatened Species
Vol. **79** Dealing with Homelessness
Vol. **80** The Cannabis Debate
Vol. **81** Alternative Therapies
Vol. **82** Protecting our Privacy
Vol. **83** Dealing with Crime
Vol. **84** Mental Wellbeing
Vol. **85** The Housing Crisis
Vol. **86** Smoking and your Health
Vol. **87** Genetic Modification
Vol. **88** Food and Nutrition
Vol. **89** Refugees
Vol. **90** Human and Animal Cloning
Vol. **91** Disability Issues

for milk proteins **90**.29-30, 32, 35
pets **90**.30, 37, 38-9
procedure **90**.27, 32, 35, 36
regulation **90**.33
religious views **90**.29
sporting animals **90**.30
X-linked inactivation **90**.37
for xeno-transplantation **90**.30, 32-3, 35
animal feed **87**.9, 11, 12-13, 27; **88**.35-6
animal research **3**.6-23
    alternatives to **3**.9, 10, 16, 19
        brain imaging techniques **3**.23
        cell and tissue culture **3**.6, 10, 22, 23
        computer modelling **3**.6, 10, 22-3
        funding **3**.22
    and anaesthetics **3**.16
    and the Animal Procedures Committee **3**.20-1
    and animal welfare **3**.10-11
    and cures for disease **3**.13
    different views on **3**.6, 12-13
    effectiveness of **3**.8-9
    European Union directive on **3**.20
    funding **3**.18
    and genetic disorders **3**.16, 18
    and healthcare advances **3**.17
    Home Office information on **3**.20-1
    and human clinical trials **3**.11
    inspectors **3**.11, 18, 20
    law on **3**.10, 16, 18, 19, 20
    moral justification of **3**.6, 9, 16
    numbers of experiments **3**.18, 19, 22
        annual statistics **3**.21
    opponents of **3**.13, 15
    origins of animals used in **3**.7
    public opinion on **3**.22
    reasons for performing **3**.8, 18, 19
    reducing **3**.16
    Refinement, Reduction and Replacement in (the three
      Rs) **3**.10, 21
    and safety of medicines **3**.6, 12, 13, 15, 17
    and similarities between animals and humans **3**.6, 11
    and suffering **3**.2, 9, 10, 16, 19, 20-1
    supporters of **3**.14
    and toxicity testing **3**.21
    types of animals used **3**.7, 16, 18, 21
    useless and irrelevant information provided by **3**.12
    validity of **3**.21
    and veterinary surgeons **3**.11, 14
    where experiments are performed **3**.7-8
animal rights **3**.1-40
    and animal welfare **3**.1-2, 4
    and the future of animals **3**.3
    and intelligence **3**.3
    and suffering **3**.2, 3
animal welfare **3**.1-4; **19**.24-40; **88**.32-3, 35-6; **90**.35
    and abattoirs **19**.25, 26, 28
    and animal experiments **3**.10-11
    and animal rights **3**.1-2, 4
    auction markets **19**.25-6, 34
    defining animal cruelty **3**.4
    European Union legislation on **19**.35, 36, 38, 39-40

and factory farming **19**.24, 30-1, 35-6, 37-8
farm buildings **19**.25
and the 'five freedoms' **19**.24, 27-8, 32, 36
humanist views on **3**.1, 2
and hunting with dogs **3**.5, 26-8, 27, 30, 31, 31-2
keeping animals healthy **19**.32-3, 36
and milk production **19**.17, 18, 30, 37
pigs **19**.25, 26, 39-40
religious views on **3**.1
slaughtering **19**.30-1
and suffering **3**.1-2
transportation of live animals **19**.25, 34-5, 36
UK legislation on **19**.24-5, 35, 36
and vegetarianism **19**.6, 24-40
views of scientists and philosophers on **3**.1
and violence in films **27**.3, 5, 34
welfare issues **19**.25
see also livestock farming; wildlife
anorexia nervosa **72**.1, 13, 15, 33; **84**.9
    age of onset **72**.17
    and attitudes to food **72**.33
    and body image **72**.36
    and bulimia **72**.15-16
    case study of **72**.18-19
    and EED (extreme eating disorder) **72**.24-5
    prevalence of **72**.16
    preventing **72**.26
    purging type **72**.22
    recovery **72**.26
    and restriction of food and calories **72**.22
    risk of developing **72**.20
    and self-harm **77**.10
    treatment **72**.26, 29
anti-depressant drugs **32**.7; **68**.13, 27, 31-2, 35-8
    in common use **68**.37
    compared with other treatments **68**.37
    and driving **68**.36
    how they work **68**.35
    lithium carbonate **68**.27
    Lustral **68**.38
    and manic depression **68**.34
    MAOIs **68**.32
    and the placebo effect **68**.35, 38
    and post-natal depression **68**.15, 16, 36
    pregnancy and breastfeeding **68**.36
    Prozac **68**.13, 27, 38
    and seasonal affective disorder **68**.21
    Seroxat **68**.38
    side effects **68**.35-6, 38
    and talking therapy **68**.38
    tricyclics **68**.35, 37, 38
    withdrawal symptoms after stopping **68**.36
antipsychotic drugs, and manic depression **68**.34
anxiety
    dealing with stress and **32**.33
    and depression **68**.1, 2, 9
    and eating disorders **72**.20
    and suicidal feelings in young people **77**.34-5
    and teenage girls **70**.31
    and work-related stress **32**.11, 20
    in young people **32**.6, 7

anxiety disorders **84.**3, 9, 16-17
    body dysmorphic disorder/dysmorphophobia **84.**16
    and childhood depression **84.**29
    generalized anxiety disorder (GAD) **84.**3, 16
    obsessive compulsive disorder (OCD) **84.**3, 9, 16
    panic disorder **84.**16
    phobias **84.**9, 16, 17
    post-traumatic stress disorder (PTSD) **84.**9, 17
    trichotillomania **84.**17
    and university students **84.**33
apples **88.**33
apprenticeship schemes **25.**19-20; **64.**9
aquifers, and global water supplies **76.**7, 16, 19
armed forces
    bullying in the Army **46.**35; **73.**34
    homeless ex-servicemen **79.**21
    and women **64.**29-32
arms sales control **55.**22
aromatherapy **81.**23, 36
    and cancer **81.**10, 33
    and multiple sclerosis **81.**30
    and the NHS **81.**4
    questions and answers **81.**10
    and scientists **81.**28, 29
    and work-related stress **32.**27
arranged marriages **40.**21-2
arsenic **86.**4
asexual reproduction **90.**2, 20
aspirin, toxicity levels compared to cannabis **80.**37
assertive behaviour **66.**28
asthma **58.**5, 15; **91.**4
asylum seekers
    in Britain *see* Britain, asylum seekers
    and child poverty **56.**17-18
    conditions for granting refugee status **89.**1
    discrimination against **63.**23
    and education **63.**11
    famous refugees **89.**1
    fleeing from conflict **89.**7-8
    and housing **85.**2, 13
    illegal immigration and identity cards **82.**2, 7, 8, 9, 10
    and marriage **40.**5

media panic over **63.**35
numbers of **89.**2, 5, 6, 10
top asylum nationalities **89.**1-2, 5, 6, 10
top countries receiving **89.**2, 5, 10
treaties and conventions **89.**3-4
and the YRE campaign **63.**39
see also refugees
athletics
    and drug testing **59.**31, 37-8
    pressures on athletes **59.**33-4
    reasons for not using drugs **59.**36
    see also drugs in sport
attempted suicide
    consequences of **77.**35
    and depression **68.**10
    factors associated with **77.**1
    and homophobic bullying in schools **73.**11
    and 'last straw' events **77.**1, 19
    ratio of attempts to completed suicide **77.**2
    and the Scottish national suicide prevention strategy **77.**20
    and subsequent suicide risk **77.**18
    support groups **77.**3
    and young men and women **77.**2, 5
    see also suicidal feelings
attendance centre orders **83.**34
attitudes *see* public attitudes
auctions
    and consumer rights **43.**17-18, 25
    online fraud **31.**39, 40
auricular acupuncture **81.**1

authoritarian parenting **67.**29
authoritative parenting **67.**29
autistic spectrum disorders **91.**26, 28
ayurveda, and cancer treatment **81.**33

B

babies
    and fathers **67.**27-8

Volume numbers appear first (in bold) followed by page numbers; a change in volume number is preceded by a semi-colon.

Vol. **3**   The Animal Rights Debate
Vol. **4**   The Euthanasia Issue
Vol. **10** Sexually Transmitted Diseases
Vol. **11** Fertility Rights
Vol. **16** Our Ageing World
Vol. **19** Looking at Vegetarianism
Vol. **20** Population Growth
Vol. **22** Confronting Child Abuse
Vol. **23** Sexuality
Vol. **25** The Changing Workplace
Vol. **27** The Censorship Issue
Vol. **28** The Global Warming Debate
Vol. **29** Gambling
Vol. **31** The Impact of the Internet
Vol. **32** Coping with Stress
Vol. **33** The Tourism Issue
Vol. **35** The Education Crisis?
Vol. **39** Alcohol Abuse
Vol. **40** The Future of Marriage
Vol. **43** A Consumer Society

Vol. **44** Confronting Domestic Violence
Vol. **46** Child Labour
Vol. **54** The Energy Debate
Vol. **55** Globalisation
Vol. **56** The Wealth Divide
Vol. **57** Waste Pollution
Vol. **58** The Transport Issue
Vol. **59** Issues in Sport
Vol. **60** Confronting Cancer
Vol. **61** Fitness
Vol. **62** Drugs and the Law
Vol. **63** The Racism Debate
Vol. **64** The Gender Issue
Vol. **65** Human Rights
Vol. **66** Self-Esteem
Vol. **67** Parenting
Vol. **68** Coping with Depression
Vol. **69** The Media
Vol. **70** Adolescent Health
Vol. **71** Abortion

Vol. **72** Obesity and Eating Disorders
Vol. **73** Dealing with Bullies
Vol. **74** Money Matters
Vol. **75** Lone-Parent Families
Vol. **76** The Water Crisis
Vol. **77** Self-inflicted Violence
Vol. **78** Threatened Species
Vol. **79** Dealing with Homelessness
Vol. **80** The Cannabis Debate
Vol. **81** Alternative Therapies
Vol. **82** Protecting our Privacy
Vol. **83** Dealing with Crime
Vol. **84** Mental Wellbeing
Vol. **85** The Housing Crisis
Vol. **86** Smoking and your Health
Vol. **87** Genetic Modification
Vol. **88** Food and Nutrition
Vol. **89** Refugees
Vol. **90** Human and Animal Cloning
Vol. **91** Disability Issues

girl babies in China **11**.26-7
infant mortality **20**.28, 29, 30, 31; **55**.21
low birthweight **56**.2
risk of homicide for **22**.14
and self-esteem **66**.1-2
sex selection of **11**.38
of teenage mothers **70**.12
    negative outcomes for **75**.2
weaning and iron in the diet **19**.5
banks
    basic bank accounts **74**.18, 24
    children and bank accounts **74**.6-7, 13
    current accounts **74**.18-19, 24
    financial education programmes for schools **74**.13
    Internet banking **74**.2
    joint bank accounts **64**.36
    money management for students **35**.39-40
    online banking **31**.3-4, 38
    overdrafts **74**.1, 18, 19, 21-2, 37
    savings accounts **74**.13, 19, 24
    and students **74**.2, 17, 21-2
        bank loans **74**.39
        choosing a bank **74**.22
        deferment period **74**.22
        graduate accounts **74**.29
        overdrafts **74**.1, 21-2, 37
        in Scotland **74**.37
        student accounts **74**.29, 32
        student debts **35**.37
    and young people **74**.9, 17-19
begging
    discouraging **79**.26, 34-5
    and yob-culture Britain **83**.5, 6
behaviour
    and children from broken homes **40**.25, 26, 27, 37
    of children witnessing domestic abuse **44**.15, 31
    disorder symptoms in young people **84**.31
    and low self-esteem **66**.6, 14, 20, 21, 29
bereavement
    and abortion **71**.25
    and adolescent health **70**.7
    and homelessness **79**.2, 32
    and mental illness **84**.28
    and self-harm **77**.30
    and suicide
        effects on families **77**.36-8
        national suicide prevention strategy **77**.19
        survivors of **77**.39
    see also funerals
biodiversity
    and climate change **28**.14-16
    and endangered animals **78**.6
    and 'England's little rainforest' **78**.34
    framework for measuring **78**.27
    and GM crops **87**.19, 30
    hot spots and population growth **20**.21
    loss of freshwater **76**.35
    and responsible tourism **33**.23, 24
    the UK and the Convention on Biological Diversity
        78.31
    and wildlife in London **85**.17

bipolar affective disorder (manic depression) **68**.9-12,
    22-3, 33-4; **84**.3, 7, 8, 20
    advice for family and friends **68**.32
    and cannabis **80**.14
    causes of **68**.23
    defining **68**.22
    diagnosis **68**.25, 33
    frequency of **68**.23, 40
    and gender **68**.23
    genetic factors **68**.20, 22, 23, 33
    and hypomania **68**.22
    manic phase **68**.19, 22, 23, 32, 33
    and suicide **77**.17-18
    symptoms **68**.19, 22, 23; **84**.9
    treatments **68**.33, 34; **84**.36
    and university students **84**.32, 33
    and violence **84**.18
birth rates
    births outside marriage **67**.6
    conception rate **11**.1, 3, 4, 11
    in developing countries **20**.1-2, 10, 38
    fall in **20**.4, 8, 16, 26, 36, 38; **40**.1
    in Germany **20**.16, 32
    low **67**.3, 33
    and population ageing **20**.15
    to teenage mothers **75**.1
    in the UK and Europe **67**.3
    see also teenage pregnancies
body image **72**.31-2
    and anabolic steroids **59**.23
    and children **72**.34
    and dieting **72**.35, 38
    and eating disorders **72**.32, 34, 36, 37
    and exercise **61**.9
    and fitness **70**.24
    influence of models on **72**.36-7
    and the media **72**.31, 34, 39
    negative **72**.32
    positive **72**.32
    and self-esteem **66**.28, 31-2; **72**.31-2
    and teenage girls **70**.31, 32, 33
Body Mass Index (BMI) **61**.14-15; **70**.29; **72**.6, 7, 12, 14,
    34; **88**.8
body weight **88**.1, 12, 18
    British people compared with Europeans **61**.16
    and eating disorders **72**.22
    and energy balance **72**.7-8
    and physical activity **61**.8-9
    and smoking **86**.25, 30, 35, 36
    weight management clinics **88**.4
    see also obesity
boys and young men
    academic performance **67**.19
    and alcohol *see* young people and alcohol
    and body image **72**.34
    and bullying **73**.5, 6
        of girls **73**.5
    and cannabis use **62**.1, 35; **80**.2, 3, 11
    and depression **68**.9
    and drug abuse **70**.14
    and eating disorders **70**.35

and education
    approach to examinations **35.**10, 11
    attainment in English **35.**6, 7, 8
    performance **64.**1, 4-8, 14, 37
    underachievement **35.**9, 10
    writing skills **35.**17
and exercise **70.**24
expenditure on the National Lottery **29.**35
and gender inequality **64.**1
and health **70.**4
    general health status **70.**1
    and happiness **70.**2
    hospital admissions **70.**6
    and tiredness **70.**3
and homophobic bullying in schools **73.**11
leaving the parental home **67.**4
life expectancy **70.**8
and physical activity **61.**2, 4; **72.**2
and pocket money **64.**13
prejudice towards gay people by **23.**17
and the prevention of teenage pregnancies **75.**23
rates of disability **91.**4
and reading **64.**2
school exclusions **64.**8
schoolchildren working illegally **25.**20
and self-esteem **66.**39
    levels of **66.**25
    and personality **66.**26
    and puberty **66.**31
sexual abuse and exploitation **46.**25-6
sexual abuse of siblings **22.**15-16
sexual behaviour **70.**10, 13; **75.**17, 18, 19, 20
and smoking **70.**18
and suicidal feelings **77.**1-2, 32-3
    and family relationships **77.**33
    and the future **77.**33
    and gender issues **77.**33
    prevention strategies **77.**33
    and schools **77.**33
and suicide **32.**8; **77.**1-2, 4, 17
    and anti-social behaviour **77.**32-3
    and depression **77.**32

    prevention **77.**23
    and waist measurement **70.**27
breast cancer **60.**3, 4, 24-5
breastfeeding
    and antidepressants **68.**36
    and teenage mothers **70.**12; **75.**2
brownfield sites
    and agricultural land **85.**28
    decontaminating **85.**22
    and new house-building **85.**9, 26, 34
    and wildlife in London **85.**16-17
bulimia nervosa **72.**13, 15; **84.**9
    age of onset **72.**17
    and anorexia **72.**15-16
    prevalence of **72.**16
    preventing **72.**26
    and purging **72.**23
    recovery **72.**26
    risk of developing **72.**20
    treatment **72.**26
bullying **22.**14; **91.**26
    body image and self-esteem **66.**32
    by neighbours **73.**1
    characteristics of bullies **73.**2
    and children's rights **65.**3
    and children's self-esteem **66.**29, 38
    compared with harassment or assault **73.**1
    crime and young people **83.**11
    defining **73.**1-2
    and girls in prison **83.**28
    health consequences of being bullied **73.**2, 6-7
    in healthcare professions **73.**1, 32-3
    homophobic **23.**18, 31, 40
    online **73.**3
    and self-harm **77.**6, 7, 9
    where people are bullied **73.**1
    in the workplace **66.**24
    of young British Army recruits **46.**35
    young men and suicidal feelings **77.**32
burglaries **83.**2, 10
    and low income households **56.**3
    rates of **83.**1, 3, 6

Volume numbers appear first (in bold) followed by page numbers; a change in volume number is preceded by a semi-colon.

Vol. **3** The Animal Rights Debate
Vol. **4** The Euthanasia Issue
Vol. **10** Sexually Transmitted Diseases
Vol. **11** Fertility Rights
Vol. **16** Our Ageing World
Vol. **19** Looking at Vegetarianism
Vol. **20** Population Growth
Vol. **22** Confronting Child Abuse
Vol. **23** Sexuality
Vol. **25** The Changing Workplace
Vol. **27** The Censorship Issue
Vol. **28** The Global Warming Debate
Vol. **29** Gambling
Vol. **31** The Impact of the Internet
Vol. **32** Coping with Stress
Vol. **33** The Tourism Issue
Vol. **35** The Education Crisis?
Vol. **39** Alcohol Abuse
Vol. **40** The Future of Marriage
Vol. **43** A Consumer Society

Vol. **44** Confronting Domestic Violence
Vol. **46** Child Labour
Vol. **54** The Energy Debate
Vol. **55** Globalisation
Vol. **56** The Wealth Divide
Vol. **57** Waste Pollution
Vol. **58** The Transport Issue
Vol. **59** Issues in Sport
Vol. **60** Confronting Cancer
Vol. **61** Fitness
Vol. **62** Drugs and the Law
Vol. **63** The Racism Debate
Vol. **64** The Gender Issue
Vol. **65** Human Rights
Vol. **66** Self-Esteem
Vol. **67** Parenting
Vol. **68** Coping with Depression
Vol. **69** The Media
Vol. **70** Adolescent Health
Vol. **71** Abortion

Vol. **72** Obesity and Eating Disorders
Vol. **73** Dealing with Bullies
Vol. **74** Money Matters
Vol. **75** Lone-Parent Families
Vol. **76** The Water Crisis
Vol. **77** Self-inflicted Violence
Vol. **78** Threatened Species
Vol. **79** Dealing with Homelessness
Vol. **80** The Cannabis Debate
Vol. **81** Alternative Therapies
Vol. **82** Protecting our Privacy
Vol. **83** Dealing with Crime
Vol. **84** Mental Wellbeing
Vol. **85** The Housing Crisis
Vol. **86** Smoking and your Health
Vol. **87** Genetic Modification
Vol. **88** Food and Nutrition
Vol. **89** Refugees
Vol. **90** Human and Animal Cloning
Vol. **91** Disability Issues

reduction targets **83**.38

buses
    bus lanes **58**.3, 14
    improvements in bus services **58**.14
    in Nottingham **58**.29
    and pollution **58**.2, 9
    public attitudes to **58**.3, 16
    school bus services **58**.3, 28
    services in other European countries **58**.16
    see also public transport

businesses
    ethics **25**.23
    investment in water-related projects **76**.28
    and rural housing **85**.28
    small businesses **55**.29; **91**.15-16
    started by older workers **16**.13, 23

C

cancer
    and alcohol consumption **39**.37; **60**.1, 15
    bladder cancer **60**.16, 17
    and blood cells **60**.34
    and body awareness **60**.18
    bone cancer **60**.9, 11, 35
    brain cancer **60**.5
    and cannabis use **80**.10, 12, 13, 26
    causes of **60**.1, 8
    cells **60**.1, 33
    cervical cancer **10**.1, 7, 11, 12; **60**.5, 14, 16
    childhood cancer **60**.8, 9-11, 13, 28, 32, 33-4
    colorectal (bowel) cancer **60**.3, 4, 6, 14, 16
    common cancer myths **60**.7-8
    and complementary therapies **60**.39; **81**.3, 10, 21, 27, 32-3
    and diet **19**.7, 15, 16; **60**.1-5, 14; **61**.13, 17, 35, 37
    early detection of **60**.36
    effects of a diagnosis of **60**.38
    and elderly people **60**.3, 7, 14
    environmental factors in **60**.1, 2
    euthanasia and terminal cancer **4**.4, 12, 15-16, 18-19, 32
    family and friends of sufferers **60**.29-30
    and family history **60**.4, 5
    inequalities in cancer incidence and mortality **60**.14
    infertility drugs and ovarian cancer **11**.6
    kidney cancer **60**.5, 9, 11, 16, 17
    leukaemia *see* leukaemia
    liver cancer **60**.5, 9, 16, 17
    lymphomas **60**.4, 9, 10, 33
    and Macmillan nurses **60**.8, 30
    and meat consumption **19**.8, 15
    melanoma (skin) cancer **28**.11-12; **60**.5, 18, 19-21
    metastases **60**.1, 8
    and milk consumption **19**.17
    mouth, lips and throat cancer **60**.5, 15
    multiple myeloma **60**.5
    and obesity **72**.6, 7, 9
    oesophageal cancer **60**.4, 15, 17
    ovarian cancer **11**.6; **60**.4, 11
    pancreatic cancer **60**.4, 16, 17

    and platelets **60**.34
    prevention **60**.2, 3; **88**.17, 30
    research **60**.2, 3
    skin cancer **28**.11-12; **60**.5, 18, 19-21
    and smoking **60**.1, 2, 3, 4, 13, 14, 15-17, 27; **86**.5, 6, 9-11, 14-16, 31
    solid cancers **60**.33
    statistics **60**.3
    stomach cancer **60**.4, 16, 17
    and sunlight **60**.1, 2
    support for people living with **60**.38
    survival rates **60**.4, 5, 13, 27
    symptoms **60**.1-2
    testicular **60**.5, 11, 12, 13, 18, 26
    thyroid cancer **60**.35
    tips for looking after yourself **60**.30
    top ten cancer killers in the UK **60**.2
    tumours **60**.1
    twenty most common cancers **60**.4-5
    and vegetarian diets **19**.19
    womb **60**.5

cancer treatments **60**.1, 4, 5
    and age of patients **60**.7, 14
    biopsies **60**.33-4
    and body scanning **60**.35, 36-7
    bone marrow transplants **60**.35, 36
    chemotherapy **60**.1, 4, 5, 26, 33, 34, 35, 36
    childhood cancer **60**.9, 33-4
    and early diagnosis **60**.7
    effectiveness of **60**.7
    epidermal growth factor receptor blockers **60**.35
    hormone therapy **60**.4, 35, 36
    and hospices **60**.8, 13
    laser treatment **60**.35
    next generation **60**.2
    nuclear medicine or isotope scanning **60**.37
    painkillers **60**.7-8
    radiotherapy **60**.1, 4, 5, 25, 33, 34, 35, 36
    surgery **60**.1, 4, 5, 26, 33-4, 35

cannabis
    and addiction **62**.31
    arguments against **80**.12
    and the cannabis economy **80**.8-9, 18
    cannabis oil **80**.1, 4, 6
    cannabis resin **80**.1, 4, 6, 7
    constituents of **80**.18
    deaths **80**.16-17, 20
    dependence on **80**.2, 12, 19, 21, 26
    and drug treatment services **62**.28
    eating **80**.1, 4, 18, 20
    effects of **80**.1-2
    and employed young adults **62**.1-2
    facts and urban myths **80**.6-7
    and footballers **59**.39
    and the gateway theory **80**.9, 26, 28
    and hard drug use **80**.9-10, 29-30
    and health **80**.7, 10, 12, 13, 15
    health risks of **62**.13, 27-8, 35
    herbal cannabis (marijuana/grass) **80**.1, 4, 6, 11
    home cultivation of **80**.32-3, 34
    and the law

arguments against liberalisation **62**.30-1, 34

classification **62**.2, 18

dealers **62**.29

decriminalisation **62**.20

growing your own **62**.18

reclassification **62**.20, 26, 27-8, 29, 35, 39

sentencing offenders **62**.22

travelling abroad **62**.19

legal position on **80**.23

legalisation debate **80**.4-6

medicinal use of **80**.5, 7, 12, 22, 34, 35-9

and mental health **80**.7, 10, 12, 13, 14, 16, 19-20, 26

and mental illness **62**.8, 27, 35; **68**.7

misconceptions **80**.9-10

names for **80**.4

as a painkiller **62**.31, 39

physical effects of **62**.2

potency of **80**.6, 11, 12, 20

prevalence of use **62**.20, 27, 28

public attitudes to **62**.39

quantity seized in the UK **62**.3

reclassification of **80**.7, 8, 14, 18, 20

risks of **62**.13, 27-8, 35; **80**.2

seizures of **80**.2, 3

side effects of **80**.2

signs of **62**.2

smoking **80**.1, 2, 4

stages of intoxication **80**.13

teenage use of **62**.1

testing for **80**.2

THC content of **80**.2, 3, 4, 6-7, 11, 13, 15, 18, 19

toxicity levels compared to aspirin **80**.37

and the treatment demand indicator (TDI) **80**.3

users

age of quitting **80**.13

and driving **80**.2, 12, 13, 16, 17, 19, 21

in EU countries **80**.3, 11

lifetime prevalence **80**.3

on negative effects of **80**.22

on positive effects of **80**.21-2

statistics on **80**.2, 3, 4, 6, 9, 18

young people in the UK **80**.11

what it looks like **80**.1, 4

where it comes from **80**.6

and young people **70**.14, 15, 16

carbohydrates **88**.2, 5-6, 15

and food labelling **88**.21, 22

carbon dioxide emissions **20**.23

and electrical appliances **54**.32, 36

and fossil fuel burning **54**.2, 4, 5, 7, 11, 12

and nuclear energy **54**.6

reducing **54**.25-6, 27

in the UK **54**.4, 10, 11, 14

see also greenhouse gas emissions

care leavers

and homelessness **79**.4, 11, 18

and teenage parenthood **75**.2

carers' needs **91**.7-8, 38

cars

abandoned **83**.5, 6

buying a cleaner car **58**.32

commuting costs **25**.10

congestion **58**.1, 4, 13

disposal of car tyres **57**.7-8

drink-driving **39**.3, 10, 18, 26, 35

drugs and driving **62**.19, 22

environmental impact of **58**.1, 5, 8-9, 9-10, 20

fuels **58**.8, 10, 35-6

and the Living Streets Campaign **58**.24-5

number of cars on the road **58**.1, 20

park and ride schemes **58**.3, 29

patterns of use **58**.6, 27

and the removal of traffic controls **58**.26

rural motorists **58**.9

school run **58**.1, 2, 19, 20, 26, 27

scrap **57**.7

social impact of car use **58**.15

traffic calming schemes **58**.16, 24, 31

casinos

age restrictions **29**.18, 27

lifting of restrictions on **29**.1, 2, 16, 17, 22

effects of **29**.2

odds on winning casino games **29**.28

online **29**.10-11, 12, 13

Volume numbers appear first (in bold) followed by page numbers; a change in volume number is preceded by a semi-colon.

Vol. **3**   The Animal Rights Debate

Vol. **4**   The Euthanasia Issue

Vol. **10** Sexually Transmitted Diseases

Vol. **11** Fertility Rights

Vol. **16** Our Ageing World

Vol. **19** Looking at Vegetarianism

Vol. **20** Population Growth

Vol. **22** Confronting Child Abuse

Vol. **23** Sexuality

Vol. **25** The Changing Workplace

Vol. **27** The Censorship Issue

Vol. **28** The Global Warming Debate

Vol. **29** Gambling

Vol. **31** The Impact of the Internet

Vol. **32** Coping with Stress

Vol. **33** The Tourism Issue

Vol. **35** The Education Crisis?

Vol. **39** Alcohol Abuse

Vol. **40** The Future of Marriage

Vol. **43** A Consumer Society

Vol. **44** Confronting Domestic Violence

Vol. **46** Child Labour

Vol. **54** The Energy Debate

Vol. **55** Globalisation

Vol. **56** The Wealth Divide

Vol. **57** Waste Pollution

Vol. **58** The Transport Issue

Vol. **59** Issues in Sport

Vol. **60** Confronting Cancer

Vol. **61** Fitness

Vol. **62** Drugs and the Law

Vol. **63** The Racism Debate

Vol. **64** The Gender Issue

Vol. **65** Human Rights

Vol. **66** Self-Esteem

Vol. **67** Parenting

Vol. **68** Coping with Depression

Vol. **69** The Media

Vol. **70** Adolescent Health

Vol. **71** Abortion

Vol. **72** Obesity and Eating Disorders

Vol. **73** Dealing with Bullies

Vol. **74** Money Matters

Vol. **75** Lone-Parent Families

Vol. **76** The Water Crisis

Vol. **77** Self-inflicted Violence

Vol. **78** Threatened Species

Vol. **79** Dealing with Homelessness

Vol. **80** The Cannabis Debate

Vol. **81** Alternative Therapies

Vol. **82** Protecting our Privacy

Vol. **83** Dealing with Crime

Vol. **84** Mental Wellbeing

Vol. **85** The Housing Crisis

Vol. **86** Smoking and your Health

Vol. **87** Genetic Modification

Vol. **88** Food and Nutrition

Vol. **89** Refugees

Vol. **90** Human and Animal Cloning

Vol. **91** Disability Issues

percentage of the population visiting **29.**7
and problem gamblers **29.**9
and social class **29.**8
celebrities
and images of self-harm **77.**7, 14
and self-esteem **66.**8, 12
censorship **27.**1.40
broadcasting **27.**2, 18-19, 40
computer games **27.**14-17
Internet **27.**1, 3, 9-13; **31.**34, 35
television **27.**7, 18, 27-9, 38-40
and television violence **69.**9
and women **27.**31-2
cereals **70.**25; **88.**5-6, 15
cervical cancer **60.**5, 14, 16
and sexually transmitted infections **10.**1, 7
smear tests **10.**11, 12
child abuse **22.**1-40
awareness of **22.**1
and care orders **22.**12
characteristics of abusers **22.**1, 4, 6
child protection conferences **22.**5
child protection registers **22.**1, 2, 11-12
deaths **22.**2, 14, 17
and domestic violence **44.**4, 15-16, 28
and eating disorders **72.**17, 20
effects of **22.**1, 4
emotional **22.**1-4, 7, 11-13
extent of **22.**10, 13-14
helplines **22.**19
neglect **22.**1, 2, 3, 4
and non-abusing family members **22.**21
physical **22.**1, 2, 4, 7, 9, 12, 13, 27
and the police **22.**5, 17
reasons for **22.**2, 8
signs and symptoms of **22.**6, 7-8
and socio-economic background **22.**3, 13, 14
statistics **22.**1-2, 3, 4, 11-12
telling someone about the abuse **22.**4-5
child labour **46.**1-18; **56.**32; **65.**15, 16-17
bonded **46.**8-9, 10
causes of **46.**1, 3
in China **46.**7-8
defining **46.**2
different type of work done by children **46.**2-3
domestic work **46.**3, 4-7, 10
geographical distribution of **65.**16-17
and governments in developing countries **46.**3, 13
hazardous work **46.**1, 10; **65.**16
long term issues in **46.**18
physical harm done by **46.**8
positive aspects of children and work **46.**1
questions and answers on **46.**2-3
solutions to **46.**17-18
statistics **65.**16
worldwide statistics on **46.**9, 10
worst forms of **46.**9-10
child pornography **22.**31-4, 37, 38, 40
and the Internet **22.**31-2, 33; **31.**27, 31, 34-6
videos **22.**33
child poverty **22.**30-1; **25.**36, 37; **40.**1

and asylum seekers **56.**17-18
and childcare **25.**36, 37
children's own accounts of **56.**9-10, 30-1, 32
defining and measuring **56.**5, 6, 7
in the developing world **56.**5, 20, 21, 26, 30-2
and disability **56.**10
and education **56.**21, 26, 30, 31, 32
effects of **56.**5
and health **56.**1
in London **85.**10
and paedophiles **22.**30-1, 33
public attitudes to **56.**20
statistics **56.**2, 4, 6
child prostitution **46.**3, 9-10, 19, 20, 27
and AIDS/HIV **46.**20, 21, 22, 26
child soldiers **46.**2, 10, 28-40; **65.**15, 22
age of recruitment **46.**30, 32, 34, 35, 38-9, 40
in Asia **46.**36, 38
background of **46.**28, 34
bullying of new recruits **46.**35
girls as **46.**10, 28, 33, 35, 37, 38, 39, 40
and international law **46.**33-4
psychological on children **46.**33, 39
reasons for joining up **46.**33
rehabilitation of **46.**37-8
sexual abuse and exploitation of **46.**21, 33, 40
and small and light weapons **46.**28, 30
towards a ban on **46.**38-9
trends of child soldiering **46.**35
turning children into soldiers **46.**33
and the UK **46.**29, 30, 32, 34, 36
voices of **46.**31
and war **46.**2, 10, 29, 30, 32
child trafficking **46.**9
and sexual exploitation and abuse **46.**19-23, 27
in the UK **46.**15, 23
in West Africa **46.**6, 7, 15
childbirth
and the baby blues **68.**9, 14
and post-natal depression **68.**9, 11, 12, 14-15, 36
childcare **25.**25-6, 33, 34-5
availability of **64.**39
costs of **25.**35, 36, 38
and grandparents **67.**4, 33
and lone parents **75.**30, 38, 39
paying grandmothers for **25.**37
statistics **25.**36
and stay-at-home fathers **67.**25, 30-1
and teenage mothers **75.**10
workers **25.**33, 36
and working fathers **64.**34, 35
and working mothers **64.**33-4, 34-5; **67.**7, 9-10, 33, 34
childless people **20.**26
high-flying women **67.**33
numbers of **67.**2
childminders
and duty of care **65.**11
and the smacking of children **22.**22, 23-4
and smoking **22.**22, 23
children
adult 'boomerang children' **67.**5

and advertising **43**.6, 7, 8, 9; **69**.11-13, 14
age and child participation **65**.21-2
age and children's rights **65**.6-7
with AIDS **10**.14, 16
alcohol consumption **39**.7, 10, 13
anti-milk campaign directed at **19**.17, 18
anxiety and phobias in **32**.7
and Attention Deficit Hyperactivity Disorder (
    ADHD) **84**.5, 29
in beanpole families **67**.5
British attitudes to **67**.7-8
cancer in childhood **60**.8, 9-11, 13, 28, 32, 33-4
in care **65**.1-2, 3, 12
and censorship
    films **27**.6-7, 25-6
    Internet **27**.10, 11-13
    R18 videos **27**.33-4
    and sex education **27**.32
    television **27**.7
of cohabiting couples **40**.2, 3, 4, 9, 10, 12-14, 20, 24;
    67.29
commercial pressure on **43**.6-8
and compulsive gambling **29**.19, 25
cruelty to animals by **3**.5
deaths of
    by violent fathers **44**.8, 30
    child abuse **22**.2, 14, 17
    mortality rates **20**.36, 40
    murders **22**.30, 31
depression in **68**.1, 4-5, 6
in developing countries
    deaths and diseases from water-related illness **76**.2,
        3, 5, 9, 13, 14
    and global water supplies **76**.13-14
    and hygiene education **76**.14
    and sanitation provision **76**.13-14
    and water collection **76**.13, 19-20
and diet **61**.34, 35-6
disciplining and physical punishment of **22**.22, 23-7
and divorce **40**.4, 15, 23-40
    parenthood as a risk factor for **67**.33
    and stepfamilies **67**.12

and domestic violence **44**.4, 5, 15, 28, 29-33
in domestic work **46**.3, 4-7, 10
and eating disorders **70**.34-6; **72**.34
and effective parenting **67**.20-1
ethnic minorities, and education **63**.11-12
explaining suicide to young children **77**.37
and fathers **67**.24-31
and food advertising **88**.10, 11, 20, 35, 37
food promotion action plan **88**.19
of gay couples **23**.37, 40; **67**.16
and globalisation **55**.1-2, 34
going missing **79**.13-14
and grandparents **67**.14-15
HIV-positive **10**.2
HIV-positive parents **10**.29
    choosing to have children **10**.30
homeless **79**.4, 8
and Internet access **31**.19-36; **69**.3
and iron deficiency **19**.5
and living wills **4**.36-7
of lone parents **40**.2, 24, 31; **67**.39; **75**.28, 29, 39
making emergency telephone calls **22**.20, 29
and mental illness **84**.1, 5-6
    diagnosis and treatment **84**.29
    and the draft mental health bill **84**.37
and mobile phone tracking **82**.19, 20
and money matters **74**.6-7, 12-13
    differences between boys and girls **74**.6, 7
    part-time jobs **74**.6
    pocket money **74**.6, 13
    spending patterns **74**.7
    teaching children about **74**.1, 5-6, 12, 13
    tweenagers **74**.4
obesity in **61**.1; **70**.29-30; **72**.4-5, 11; **88**.3, 11
    and bedroom TVs **61**.5
    and diabetes **61**.1, 6, 7, 11, 12
    and diet **61**.17, 35
    and heart disease **61**.6
of older parents **67**.36-7
parents making time for **67**.20-1, 38-9
parents and stress in children **32**.8, 10
and parents who drink too much **39**.14, 30-2

Volume numbers appear first (in bold) followed by page numbers; a change in volume number is preceded by a semi-colon.

Vol. 3   The Animal Rights Debate
Vol. 4   The Euthanasia Issue
Vol. 10   Sexually Transmitted Diseases
Vol. 11   Fertility Rights
Vol. 16   Our Ageing World
Vol. 19   Looking at Vegetarianism
Vol. 20   Population Growth
Vol. 22   Confronting Child Abuse
Vol. 23   Sexuality
Vol. 25   The Changing Workplace
Vol. 27   The Censorship Issue
Vol. 28   The Global Warming Debate
Vol. 29   Gambling
Vol. 31   The Impact of the Internet
Vol. 32   Coping with Stress
Vol. 33   The Tourism Issue
Vol. 35   The Education Crisis?
Vol. 39   Alcohol Abuse
Vol. 40   The Future of Marriage
Vol. 43   A Consumer Society

Vol. 44   Confronting Domestic Violence
Vol. 46   Child Labour
Vol. 54   The Energy Debate
Vol. 55   Globalisation
Vol. 56   The Wealth Divide
Vol. 57   Waste Pollution
Vol. 58   The Transport Issue
Vol. 59   Issues in Sport
Vol. 60   Confronting Cancer
Vol. 61   Fitness
Vol. 62   Drugs and the Law
Vol. 63   The Racism Debate
Vol. 64   The Gender Issue
Vol. 65   Human Rights
Vol. 66   Self-Esteem
Vol. 67   Parenting
Vol. 68   Coping with Depression
Vol. 69   The Media
Vol. 70   Adolescent Health
Vol. 71   Abortion

Vol. 72   Obesity and Eating Disorders
Vol. 73   Dealing with Bullies
Vol. 74   Money Matters
Vol. 75   Lone-Parent Families
Vol. 76   The Water Crisis
Vol. 77   Self-inflicted Violence
Vol. 78   Threatened Species
Vol. 79   Dealing with Homelessness
Vol. 80   The Cannabis Debate
Vol. 81   Alternative Therapies
Vol. 82   Protecting our Privacy
Vol. 83   Dealing with Crime
Vol. 84   Mental Wellbeing
Vol. 85   The Housing Crisis
Vol. 86   Smoking and your Health
Vol. 87   Genetic Modification
Vol. 88   Food and Nutrition
Vol. 89   Refugees
Vol. 90   Human and Animal Cloning
Vol. 91   Disability Issues

finding someone to talk to **39**.31-2
   looking for signs **39**.33
and passive smoking **60**.17
playing on the street **58**.25, 26
and poverty *see* child poverty
in prison (under 18s) **83**.23, 27-9
and racism **63**.1-2
and radio, taste and decency on **69**.36-7
refugees **89**.39
relationships with separated fathers **75**.36
and road accidents **58**.1, 15, 20, 26
schoolchildren working illegally **25**.20-1
sedentary lifestyles **61**.1, 3, 8, 10
and self-esteem **66**.1-2
   advice for parents on **66**.36, 39
   backhanded praise **66**.36
   confident children and social ills **66**.38
   developing **66**.12-14, 29-30
   improving **66**.27-8
   overpraising **66**.36, 37-8
   praising appropriate behaviour **66**.8-9, 36
   and undeserved praise **66**.21
and sex stereotyping **64**.37
sexual abuse *see* sexual abuse
sexual pressures on **23**.24-5
smacking **22**.22, 23-4, 26; **65**.7, 12, 13-14, 14; **67**.31
and smoking **70**.18-19; **86**.1, 8, 14-15, 24-5, 26
and spam (Unsolicited Bulk Emails) **82**.31
in stepfamilies **40**.2, 25, 31-2, 34, 36, 37; **67**.12, 13
and sun exposure **60**.19, 20-1
of teenage mothers **70**.12; **75**.2, 7-8
and television
   and the 9 p.m. watershed **69**.10
   advertising **69**.11-13
   BARB genre classifications **69**.7
   children's programmes **69**.3, 5, 6
   multichannel **69**.5-6
   programme content regulation **69**.2, 10
   and programme origination **69**.6
   protection of children **69**.3
   soap operas **69**.8
   What Children Watch **69**.5-7
travelling in cars **58**.2, 5, 21
and vegetarian diets **19**.1
and working mothers **67**.32, 34-5, 38-9
children's rights **65**.1-23
and age of children **65**.6-7
basic beliefs behind **65**.6
and child participation **65**.21-2, 23
and child slaves **65**.34
and child soldiers **65**.15, 22
children lecturing MPs on **65**.3
and children's needs **65**.7
Commissioners **65**.3, 9-10
defining **65**.6
donor-conceived children and identity of biological
   parents **65**.8-9
and early marriage **65**.18, 19, 20
and the Gillick principle **65**.11, 12
and girls in developing countries **65**.18, 19-20

Government policies on **65**.7
instructing solicitors **65**.7
legislation **65**.7, 10, 11
and the media **65**.1, 3, 4
personal rights **65**.1
and physical punishment **65**.7, 12, 13-14
questions about **65**.6-7
and respect for adults **65**.7
and responsibilities **65**.6
sexual exploitation and the human rights of girls **65**.19
in the UK **65**.7
Chinese medicine **81**.2, 3
and cancer **81**.33
and endangered species **81**.15
herbal medicine **81**.14-15, 39
chiropractic **81**.8-9, 23, 36
and back pain **81**.9
defining **81**.1, 8
effectiveness of **81**.24
misdiagnosis and dangers of **81**.23, 24
and the neck **81**.9
and the NHS **81**.4
regulation of **81**.23
and scientists **81**.28, 29
and the spine **81**.8-9
cholesterol
and coronary heart disease **19**.10, 19
and egg consumption **19**.16
and smoking **86**.10
and vegetarian diets **19**.15, 20
cigarettes
and cannabis users **80**.26
chemicals in **86**.4, 9-10
deaths caused by **80**.10
development of cannabis **80**.9
flavourings in **86**.7
herbal **86**.37
low tar **86**.32
see also smoking
cigars **86**.36
citizenship **35**.1; **89**.37
civil liberties
and the cannabis legalisation debate **80**.5
and Internet censorship **27**.9
civil marriages **40**.3, 5, 13, 15
and the law **40**.14, 17-18, 19, 20
as a percentage of all marriages **40**.19
CJD (Creutzfeldt-Jakob disease) **16**.37
claustrophobia **84**.16, 17
climate change **54**.2, 5, 10, 14
and biodiversity **28**.14-16
causes of **28**.1, 7, 29-30, 35
and cleaner cars **58**.34, 35
and disease **28**.7, 10, 12, 30
drought **28**.7, 9, 12, 15, 26
energy politics **54**.19, 25, 35-6
evidence for **28**.38
and floods **28**.9, 10, 12, 15, 20, 23, 26
food production **28**.13, 26
and global water supplies **76**.1, 3, 5, 8
and the Gulf Stream **28**.4, 11, 12, 28

impacts of **28**.40

permafrost melting **28**.15

sceptics and research on **28**.19, 21, 22

scientists' predictions **28**.10-11

and the seasons **28**.16

and species extinction **78**.10, 11

storms and hurricanes **28**.7, 9, 15, 26, 30

temperature rises **28**.1, 15, 17, 20, 21, 22, 23, 25, 29, 31, 38

and traffic pollution **58**.1, 5, 8-9, 32

in the UK **28**.12-13, 17, 28

and water management **76**.34

cloning **11**.31

clothes

recycling **57**.35-6

shopping **43**.5, 8, 11

cocaine

and employed young adults **62**.1

and the law

classification **62**.2, 18

treatment services **62**.16

physical effects of **62**.2

prevalence of use **62**.4, 7

quantity seized in the UK **62**.3

signs of **62**.2

use by young people **80**.2

see also crack cocaine

cohabiting couples

children of **40**.2-4, 9-10, 12-14, 20, 24; **67**.29

and the law **40**.14, 18

length of relationships **40**.2

numbers of **40**.2, 4

and physical aggression **40**.10

risk of breakup **40**.6-7, 9, 10

statistics **20**.26

and young people **40**.4, 6

colleges

and drug use **62**.18

self-esteem of students **66**.18-19

students and mental illness **84**.32-3

communities

and children's rights **65**.2

and identity cards **82**.11

and mental health, positive steps to **84**.27

sustainable **85**.32, 38, 39

values and broadcasting regulation **27**.18

community sentences **83**.34

and young offenders **83**.13, 16, 24-5, 30

commuting

stress **25**.10-11, 27; **32**.36-7

complaints

about children and advertising **43**.9

about goods and services **43**.22

about utilities **43**.23

rise in consumer **43**.19

sources of help **43**.22-3

complementary medicine (CM)

and animal research **3**.22

and cancer **60**.39

choosing a therapy **81**.4

and consumer choice **81**.37

and consumer ignorance **81**.35

defining **81**.1, 4

and depression **68**.27

and diagnosis **81**.34

disciplines within **81**.1-3

effectiveness of **81**.22-4, 26, 27, 31

expenditure on **81**.23, 37, 39

'feelgood' counselling effect of **81**.29

and the Foundation for Integrated Health **81**.29, 36

global strategy on **81**.39

and GPs **81**.21

and HIV **10**.32

impact on wildlife **78**.23

and misdiagnosis **81**.23

and multiple sclerosis **81**.30-1

and the placebo effect **81**.26, 28, 34

questions to ask the practitioner **81**.4

regulation of **81**.23

safety of **81**.27, 31

and scientists **81**.28-9

and seasonal affective disorder **68**.21

and self-care **81**.36-7

why bogus therapies seem to work **81**.34

Volume numbers appear first (in bold) followed by page numbers; a change in volume number is preceded by a semi-colon.

Vol. 3   The Animal Rights Debate

Vol. 4   The Euthanasia Issue

Vol. 10 Sexually Transmitted Diseases

Vol. 11 Fertility Rights

Vol. 16 Our Ageing World

Vol. 19 Looking at Vegetarianism

Vol. 20 Population Growth

Vol. 22 Confronting Child Abuse

Vol. 23 Sexuality

Vol. 25 The Changing Workplace

Vol. 27 The Censorship Issue

Vol. 28 The Global Warming Debate

Vol. 29 Gambling

Vol. 31 The Impact of the Internet

Vol. 32 Coping with Stress

Vol. 33 The Tourism Issue

Vol. 35 The Education Crisis?

Vol. 39 Alcohol Abuse

Vol. 40 The Future of Marriage

Vol. 43 A Consumer Society

Vol. 44 Confronting Domestic Violence

Vol. 46 Child Labour

Vol. 54 The Energy Debate

Vol. 55 Globalisation

Vol. 56 The Wealth Divide

Vol. 57 Waste Pollution

Vol. 58 The Transport Issue

Vol. 59 Issues in Sport

Vol. 60 Confronting Cancer

Vol. 61 Fitness

Vol. 62 Drugs and the Law

Vol. 63 The Racism Debate

Vol. 64 The Gender Issue

Vol. 65 Human Rights

Vol. 66 Self-Esteem

Vol. 67 Parenting

Vol. 68 Coping with Depression

Vol. 69 The Media

Vol. 70 Adolescent Health

Vol. 71 Abortion

Vol. 72 Obesity and Eating Disorders

Vol. 73 Dealing with Bullies

Vol. 74 Money Matters

Vol. 75 Lone-Parent Families

Vol. 76 The Water Crisis

Vol. 77 Self-inflicted Violence

Vol. 78 Threatened Species

Vol. 79 Dealing with Homelessness

Vol. 80 The Cannabis Debate

Vol. 81 Alternative Therapies

Vol. 82 Protecting our Privacy

Vol. 83 Dealing with Crime

Vol. 84 Mental Wellbeing

Vol. 85 The Housing Crisis

Vol. 86 Smoking and your Health

Vol. 87 Genetic Modification

Vol. 88 Food and Nutrition

Vol. 89 Refugees

Vol. 90 Human and Animal Cloning

Vol. 91 Disability Issues

for work-related stress **32**.27
see also Chinese medicine
composting waste **57**.18, 19, 21, 22, 33, 35, 39
    making your own compost **57**.24-5, 35
    worm composting **57**.21, 24, 25
compulsive gambling **29**.18-40
    abstinence or control **29**.30, 31
    advice on controlling **29**.20, 39-40
    asking questions about **29**.25, 30, 31-3
    and betting games **29**.35
    and children **29**.19, 25
    company levies to pay for treatment **29**.36
    consequences of **29**.27-8
    defining **29**.31, 39
    dream world of the compulsive gambler **29**.33
    families and what to do **29**.28
    and fruit machines **29**.35, 36
    online **29**.14, 19
    overcoming **29**.29-30
    periodic **29**.32
    personal experiences of **29**.22
    and personality traits **29**.32-3, 39
    prevalence of **29**.1-2
    profile of problem gamblers **29**.9
    reasons for addiction **29**.27
    relapse-prevention strategy **29**.30
    signs and symptoms of **29**.24-5, 27, 29-30
    and television **29**.19
    and UK gambling law reforms **29**.16, 17, 18-19, 22-3
    in the United States **29**.37-8
    and willpower **29**.31-2
    and young people **29**.2, 19, 37-8
computer games **27**.14-17
    new age rating symbols for **27**.14-15
    parents suing computer games companies **27**.17
computers
    hackers and credit card fraud **31**.38
    home computer use **40**.1; **43**.2
        and occupational group **25**.2
        and people in their 50s **16**.8, 9
    and older business owners **16**.23
    personal computer ownership **69**.1, 2
    recycling **57**.33
    in schools **31**.5, 8; **35**.25
    use of laptop PCs **31**.3
    viruses **31**.13
condoms **75**.15, 16, 17, 22
    avoiding sexually transmitted infections **10**.4, 6, 9, 10
    and gay men **10**.2
    and genital herpes **10**.8
    and genital warts **10**.7-8, 12
    protecting against HIV **10**.22, 27
    and sex education **75**.22
    and teenage sex **75**.17
    and worldwide AIDS/HIV prevention programmes
        10.36, 37, 38
conservation
    animal species **78**.11
    and the exotic pet trade **78**.21-2
    and foxhunting **3**.38-9
    plant species **78**.17

    sparrows **78**.37
    tree species **78**.12
    zoo conservation **78**.24-5
consumer rights **43**.16-18
    and extended warranties **43**.20-1
    faulty presents **43**.17, 25
    limits to **43**.25
    private sales and auctions **43**.17-18, 25
    secondhand goods **43**.25
    unfair contract terms **43**.18
consumer spending
    boycotts **43**.4
    and children **43**.6-8
    expenditure patterns **43**.1, 2, 3-4
    and family pets **3**.5
    and globalisation **43**.10-11
    insights into consumer markets **43**.3-4
    and the over 50s **16**.10
    spending spree **43**.1, 8
    and viral marketing **43**.12
consumers
    awareness surveys **43**.14, 15-16
    and cannabis economy **80**.8-9
    complaints **43**.9, 19, 22-3
consumption
    and the gap between rich and poor **56**.12
    increase in **55**.29
    lifestyle choices and fairer trade **55**.30
    and the measurement of poverty **56**.23
    and population growth **20**.8, 22-3, 24
contraception **75**.15-16
    after an abortion **71**.2, 7, 10
    emergency contraception (EC) **75**.3, 13, 15-16, 17
    failure of **71**.28
    and family planning services **75**.16
    in India **20**.30
    and the male pill **20**.38-9
    obtaining **71**.13
    and population growth **20**.3
    sterilization **75**.15, 16
    and teenagers **10**.2; **70**.10, 13
    and under-16s **71**.11, 28-9
    vasectomies **75**.16
    and women 'at risk' of pregnancy **75**.15
    and young people **75**.2-3, 13
corporal punishment
    and children's rights **65**.7, 13-14
    and teachers **65**.15
cot death **86**.25
counselling
    for abusive men **44**.38-9
    HIV-positive people **10**.29
    and mental illness **84**.10
    post-abortion **71**.27, 31, 34
    and school bullying **73**.24
    and seasonal affective disorder **68**.21
    students and counselling services **84**.32, 33
    as a treatment for depression **68**.13, 27, 31, 37, 39
    for victims of domestic violence **44**.3, 9, 21
    and work-related stress **32**.20, 26, 28
    and workplace bullying **73**.37, 38

and young people **84**.24, 31-2
countryside
effects of air transport **58**.17-18
see also rural areas; rural housing
courts of law
and arranged marriages **40**.22
children and divorce **40**.23, 30-1
and debts **74**.35
and domestic violence **44**.23, 30, 39, 40
and the media **69**.38
crack cocaine
and patterns of drug use **62**.4, 9, 14
quantity seized in the UK **62**.3
treatment programmes **62**.16, 17
see also cocaine
credit
advantages and disadvantages of **74**.23
bank overdrafts **74**.1, 18, 19, 21-2
brokers' fees **43**.32
buying on **43**.29, 31
cancelling a credit agreement **43**.32
credit ratings **74**.25, 27
extra protection when using **43**.32
interest rates **74**.23
obtaining **74**.23
reference agencies **43**.31-2
settling up early **43**.32-3
and students **74**.30
see also debt
credit cards **74**.26-7
card-not-present fraud **43**.26
and the cashless society **74**.9-11
chip cards **43**.34-5
credit reference agencies **74**.25, 27
fraud **43**.26-7, 28
and home shopping **82**.36
interest rates **43**.28; **74**.26, 27
international card payment schemes **74**.26
limits **74**.26
minimum repayments **74**.26
'payment holidays' **74**.26
shopping around for **74**.25-6

store cards **74**.27
and students **74**.3, 30, 32, 36, 37
theft, and RFID tags **82**.16
and under 18s **43**.23-4
use of **43**.28
and young people **74**.15, 16, 23
crime
and alcohol **39**.3, 6, 8, 14, 18, 19, 24
and anti-social behaviour **79**.26
attitudes to criminal activities **43**.4
and children of lone parents **75**.29
compensation for criminal injuries and deaths **23**.37
and drug abuse **80**.28
drug-related **62**.36, 39
fear of **56**.3, 14; **83**.6
and gambling **29**.1, 17, 22
housing and the environment **85**.14
and identity cards
forging **82**.7, 8
as a means of combating crime **82**.7, 8, 10, 11
and low income households **56**.3
and mental illness **84**.4
and police stop and search practices **63**.33
racial violence **63**.4, 7, 13-15, 28-9
rates **83**.1-2, 3, 13, 14
and RFID cards **82**.17
in rural areas **83**.2
statistics **83**.1-2, 3, 6
students as victims of **35**.34
and surveillance **82**.17-18
and teenage parenthood **75**.2
victims of **83**.6, 7, 14
and violence on television **27**.35-6
wildlife **78**.19, 38-9
and women **64**.39
and yob-culture Britain **83**.5-6
crime prevention **83**.31-9
criminal justice system
and children's rights **65**.2, 5
and ethnic minorities **63**.17-18, 33
and the Human Rights Act **65**.24
race crimes and the Crown Prosecution Service **63**.37

Volume numbers appear first (in bold) followed by page numbers; a change in volume number is preceded by a semi-colon.

Vol. **3** The Animal Rights Debate
Vol. **4** The Euthanasia Issue
Vol. **10** Sexually Transmitted Diseases
Vol. **11** Fertility Rights
Vol. **16** Our Ageing World
Vol. **19** Looking at Vegetarianism
Vol. **20** Population Growth
Vol. **22** Confronting Child Abuse
Vol. **23** Sexuality
Vol. **25** The Changing Workplace
Vol. **27** The Censorship Issue
Vol. **28** The Global Warming Debate
Vol. **29** Gambling
Vol. **31** The Impact of the Internet
Vol. **32** Coping with Stress
Vol. **33** The Tourism Issue
Vol. **35** The Education Crisis?
Vol. **39** Alcohol Abuse
Vol. **40** The Future of Marriage
Vol. **43** A Consumer Society

Vol. **44** Confronting Domestic Violence
Vol. **46** Child Labour
Vol. **54** The Energy Debate
Vol. **55** Globalisation
Vol. **56** The Wealth Divide
Vol. **57** Waste Pollution
Vol. **58** The Transport Issue
Vol. **59** Issues in Sport
Vol. **60** Confronting Cancer
Vol. **61** Fitness
Vol. **62** Drugs and the Law
Vol. **63** The Racism Debate
Vol. **64** The Gender Issue
Vol. **65** Human Rights
Vol. **66** Self-Esteem
Vol. **67** Parenting
Vol. **68** Coping with Depression
Vol. **69** The Media
Vol. **70** Adolescent Health
Vol. **71** Abortion

Vol. **72** Obesity and Eating Disorders
Vol. **73** Dealing with Bullies
Vol. **74** Money Matters
Vol. **75** Lone-Parent Families
Vol. **76** The Water Crisis
Vol. **77** Self-inflicted Violence
Vol. **78** Threatened Species
Vol. **79** Dealing with Homelessness
Vol. **80** The Cannabis Debate
Vol. **81** Alternative Therapies
Vol. **82** Protecting our Privacy
Vol. **83** Dealing with Crime
Vol. **84** Mental Wellbeing
Vol. **85** The Housing Crisis
Vol. **86** Smoking and your Health
Vol. **87** Genetic Modification
Vol. **88** Food and Nutrition
Vol. **89** Refugees
Vol. **90** Human and Animal Cloning
Vol. **91** Disability Issues

and restorative justice **83.**37-8
and the Universal Declaration of Human Rights **65.**29
see also courts of law; youth justice
criticism
    and body image **66.**32
    and self-esteem **66.**27
culture
    effects on body image and self-esteem **66.**31-2
    impacts of tourism **33.**31
    and responsible tourism **33.**26

D

data protection
    communications data **82.**33-4
    EU rules on **82.**3, 5
    and RFID tags **82.**16
    and self-regulation **82.**5
deaths **20.**25, 27, 30
    abortion-related **20.**25, 27, 30; **71.**16
    accidental deaths of children **56.**2
    in adolescence **70.**3, 6
    from AIDS/HIV **10.**1, 14-17, 21, 26, 27, 33, 35
    alcohol-related **39.**1, 5, 6, 9, 15, 18, 34
    cancer **60.**3, 7, 27
    from cancer **81.**23, 32
    cancer
        fall in **60.**13
        and hospices **60.**8
        lung cancer **60.**3, 15, 27
        and painkillers **60.**8
        skin cancer **60.**19
        and smoking **60.**15, 27
    of children
        by violent fathers **44.**8, 30
        child abuse **22.**2, 14, 17
        in the developing world **56.**28
        mortality rates **20.**36, 40
        murders **22.**30, 31
    compensation for criminal injuries and deaths **23.**37
    and drug misuse **80.**10, 11
    from eating disorders **72.**23
    fall in death rates **20.**2
    from smoking **86.**2, 9, 10, 14, 16, 17
    from heart disease **61.**4
    homeless people **79.**32
    from illegal drug use **62.**7
    infant mortality **20.**28, 29, 30, 31; **56.**4, 28, 35, 37
    maternal mortality **20.**25, 28, 29, 30, 36, 37, 39
    missing persons **79.**14
    obesity-related **70.**29; **72.**5, 12
    premature deaths in the UK **56.**1
    in road accidents **58.**1, 20, 26
    rough sleepers **79.**15
    from water-related diseases **76.**2, 9, 13, 14, 20, 35
    'winter excess' in the UK **85.**37
    see also bereavement; funerals
debit cards **43.**24, 29
    and bank accounts **74.**18
    and the cashless society **74.**9-11

and young people **74.**23-4
debt
    attitudes to **74.**5
    buying on credit **43.**29
    calculating total repayments **74.**26
    communication with creditors **74.**25
    counselling **43.**30
    defining **55.**4
    developing countries **55.**34, 37
    and families **74.**3, 5-6
    getting out of **74.**16
    and lone parents **75.**37, 38
    managing **74.**34-5
    National Debt Line **74.**25
    and poverty in the developing world **56.**21, 22, 26
    profile of individuals with debt problems **43.**30-1
    rise in personal debt **43.**2
    and secured loans **74.**25
    seeking help with **43.**33-4
    students **35.**27, 29, 32-9; **74.**3, 5, 19-20, 31-2, 34-9
    tips for cutting **74.**25-6
    and unauthorised money lenders **74.**24
    women and debt problems **43.**30-1, 38-9
    and young people **74.**1, 2, 15, 16, 23
    see also credit
deforestation
    and global warming **28.**8, 9, 10, 11
    and paper making **57.**34
    and population growth **20.**1, 14, 23, 24
    and trade liberalisation **55.**29
    and water shortages **76.**21, 36
dementia **16.**30, 33, 34, 36-9
    Alzheimer's disease **84.**11-12
    causes of **84.**12
    missing persons suffering from **79.**13, 14
    specialist services for people with **16.**39
    statistics on **16.**37
    symptoms of **84.**12
    types of **16.**36-7
democracy
    and corporate globalisation **55.**16
    global **55.**23-4
    and the Human Rights Act **65.**26
    and the Internet **55.**1
    and the National Curriculum **35.**1
    and the World Trade Organisation **55.**11-12
depression **84.**6-7
    and abortion **71.**33, 35
    and adolescent health **70.**1, 2, 6, 8
    advice for family and friends **68.**32
    and alcohol misuse **39.**16
    anti-depressant drugs **84.**35-6
    and anxiety **68.**9
    attitudes to **84.**19-20, 21
    and cannabis **62.**8; **80.**7, 16, 22
    causes of **68.**4, 6, 19-20; **84.**6
    in childhood **84.**29
    in children and young people **40.**34; **44.**15; **68.**6, 9, 28-31
    clinical **84.**9
    and complementary medicine **81.**30, 31

complications 68.27
defining 68.1, 9, 12, 18
diagnosing 68.24-5, 26-7
and domestic violence 44.2
drug treatment for 84.19
and eating disorders 72.16, 20
endogenous 68.18-19
frequency of 68.1, 9, 11
genetic factors in 68.9-10, 20
getting help 84.7
and homeless young people 79.33, 36
and low self-esteem 66.3, 10, 12, 13, 14
manic depression *see* bipolar affective disorder
neurotic 68.18
numbers of adults suffering from 68.1
and personality 68.11
and physical activity 61.11, 19; 70.5
post-natal 84.9
questions and answers 68.9-10
reactive 68.18, 20
recovery from 68.10
recurrence and relapse 68.10
reducing the risk of 68.12-13
resistant 68.10
secondary 68.19
severe (clinical) depression 68.12
the 'smiling depressive' 84.20
statistics on 84.1
and stress 68.1, 2-3
and suicide 77.3
symptoms of 68.1-2, 11, 17, 26-7; 84.3, 4, 6-7
and teenage girls 70.31
treatment for 84.35-6
treatment of 68.10, 26-39
types of 68.18-19; 84.7
unipolar (endogenous) 68.9, 18-19, 20
and work performance 84.23
and work-related stress 32.11, 20, 28
and workplace bullying 73.33
developing countries
age discrimination in employment 16.22
ageing population 20.9, 11

aid to 55.4, 38; 56.35-6
children and water collection 76.13-14
complementary medicine in 81.39
early marriage in 65.18, 19, 20, 35
economic growth 56.1, 37
education in 20.20, 28
financial flows to 55.36
and global warming 28.27, 39
and globalisation 55.1-2, 12-13, 14-15, 35-6
and GM crops 87.3, 4, 7, 28-30, 36
governments and 'poverty reduction strategies' 56.35
international tourist chains in 33.5
and international trade 55.31-2, 33-4, 35-6
life expectancy 16.29; 20.5
malnutrition and adult obesity in 61.7
obesity in 72.10
older people in 16.4, 7, 10
population growth 20.1-2, 4, 5, 8-9, 10
poverty in 56.5, 21-2, 26, 35-6
and pro-poor tourism 33.34-5
and responsible tourism 33.18, 32-3
and the right to water 76.24-5, 32
sedentary lifestyles in 61.11
shantytowns 20.17-18, 20
slavery 65.34-5
and structural adjustment policies 55.2, 10, 34
and teleworking 25.9
and the tourism boom 33.38-40
and transnational companies 55.27
urban growth 20.9, 11, 17-20, 33
water collection 76.13, 19-20
water pollution 76.4, 10
water and sanitation services 76.7, 8, 12, 17, 21
water shortages 76.16, 19, 21
women's rights 65.33
young people 20.10-11, 33-4, 40
diabetes
in adolescents 70.3, 27, 28
and complementary therapies 81.21
and food nutrition 88.9
and obesity 61.12, 15; 72.1, 4-8, 11
and physical activity 61.26

Volume numbers appear first (in bold) followed by page numbers; a change in volume number is preceded by a semi-colon.

Vol. 3 The Animal Rights Debate
Vol. 4 The Euthanasia Issue
Vol. 10 Sexually Transmitted Diseases
Vol. 11 Fertility Rights
Vol. 16 Our Ageing World
Vol. 19 Looking at Vegetarianism
Vol. 20 Population Growth
Vol. 22 Confronting Child Abuse
Vol. 23 Sexuality
Vol. 25 The Changing Workplace
Vol. 27 The Censorship Issue
Vol. 28 The Global Warming Debate
Vol. 29 Gambling
Vol. 31 The Impact of the Internet
Vol. 32 Coping with Stress
Vol. 33 The Tourism Issue
Vol. 35 The Education Crisis?
Vol. 39 Alcohol Abuse
Vol. 40 The Future of Marriage
Vol. 43 A Consumer Society

Vol. 44 Confronting Domestic Violence
Vol. 46 Child Labour
Vol. 54 The Energy Debate
Vol. 55 Globalisation
Vol. 56 The Wealth Divide
Vol. 57 Waste Pollution
Vol. 58 The Transport Issue
Vol. 59 Issues in Sport
Vol. 60 Confronting Cancer
Vol. 61 Fitness
Vol. 62 Drugs and the Law
Vol. 63 The Racism Debate
Vol. 64 The Gender Issue
Vol. 65 Human Rights
Vol. 66 Self-Esteem
Vol. 67 Parenting
Vol. 68 Coping with Depression
Vol. 69 The Media
Vol. 70 Adolescent Health
Vol. 71 Abortion

Vol. 72 Obesity and Eating Disorders
Vol. 73 Dealing with Bullies
Vol. 74 Money Matters
Vol. 75 Lone-Parent Families
Vol. 76 The Water Crisis
Vol. 77 Self-inflicted Violence
Vol. 78 Threatened Species
Vol. 79 Dealing with Homelessness
Vol. 80 The Cannabis Debate
Vol. 81 Alternative Therapies
Vol. 82 Protecting our Privacy
Vol. 83 Dealing with Crime
Vol. 84 Mental Wellbeing
Vol. 85 The Housing Crisis
Vol. 86 Smoking and your Health
Vol. 87 Genetic Modification
Vol. 88 Food and Nutrition
Vol. 89 Refugees
Vol. 90 Human and Animal Cloning
Vol. 91 Disability Issues

research **90.**18, 23-4
diet **61.**29-37
   of adolescents **70.**25-6
   British schoolchildren **72.**37
   and cancer **60.**1-5, 14; **61.**13, 37
   and cancer treatments **81.**32-3
   carbohydrates **61.**32-3, 34
   and children **61.**34, 35-6
   controlling stress through **32.**31, 35, 38-9
   and depression **68.**12-13, 17
   essential fatty acids **61.**37
   fat in the diet **61.**30-1, 34, 37
   fruit and vegetables **61.**30, 32, 34
   and health **61.**13, 30
   and homeopathy **81.**13
   iron in the diet **19.**3, 5, 8
   making dietary changes **61.**31
   nutrition research and media stories **61.**18
   and obesity **61.**7, 8
   salt in the diet **61.**34
   and schizophrenia **84.**14-15
   snacks and blood sugar levels **61.**33
   sugary foods **61.**33, 34
   and weight loss
   and young people **61.**1
dieting
   advice for teenagers **72.**13-14
   and body image **70.**33; **72.**32, 38
   danger signs **72.**14
   and energy balance **72.**7-8
   girls and self-esteem **66.**11, 31
   girls and young women **72.**2, 13, 35
   and healthy eating **72.**38
   and weight loss **72.**13
   and women **72.**38
disabled children **91.**4, 18, 28, 29-30
disabled people
   adolescents **70.**6, 8
   disclosing a disability **91.**19
   discrimination **91.**5, 6, 7, 12-25
   and domestic violence **44.**3
   economic independence **91.**11
   and education **91.**7, 10, 29-36
   and employment **91.**3, 4, 7, 10, 15-16, 19-20, 32
   famous disabled people **91.**3, 22
   health provision **91.**11, 37-8, 39
   housing **91.**11, 17
   identity **91.**28
   information provision **91.**11, 12
   paying extra for rights of **91.**3
   and poverty **56.**2
   public attitudes to disability **91.**2-4
   purchasing power **91.**14
   quality of life **91.**9
   service and goods provision **91.**7, 8, 13-14
   and soap operas **69.**8-9
   students and state benefits **74.**39
   supplying cannabis to **80.**33
   tribunal claims **91.**12
   wheelchair students **91.**36
discrimination

   in the Army **73.**34
   and children's rights **65.**1, 15
   defining **63.**27
   direct and indirect **63.**4, 27
   of disabled people **91.**5, 6, 7, 12-25
   legal protection against discrimination in the workplace **73.**37
   against lesbian and gay employees **23.**32-5
   and mental illness **84.**19-20, 21-2
   and Muslims in the UK **63.**22-3
   and obese people **72.**9
   positive **63.**4, 8
   religious **63.**21
   and reproductive technology **11.**32
   and sex stereotyping **64.**37
   and the Universal Declaration of Human Rights **65.**29
   and women at work **64.**10, 11
   and women's rights **65.**33
disease
   and climate change **28.**7, 10, 12, 30
   diabetes in children **61.**1, 6, 7, 11, 12, 35
   and diet **19.**15, 19
   and illness in adolescence **70.**6
   and lack of physical activity **61.**1, 11
   and obesity **61.**12
   and poor sexual health **10.**1
   and population growth **20.**6, 19, 20
   and poverty **56.**1, 30, 31
   prevention and treatment of farm livestock **19.**32-3, 36
   and unhealthy diets **61.**13, 30
   water-related **76.**2, 3, 5, 6, 9, 12, 119, 20, 35
divorce
   attitudes to **67.**1
   changing attitudes to **40.**40
   and changing trends in family life **40.**3
   and children **40.**4, 15, 23-40; **67.**12
   and the costs of family breakdown **40.**25
   and fathers **25.**32; **65.**11
   length of marriages ending in divorce **40.**18
   and lone parents **75.**28, 31, 33
   parenthood as a risk factor for **67.**33
   and parenting **67.**17
   rates **40.**3, 4, 15, 25, 28, 29; **67.**18
   religious views on **40.**28
   and remarriage **40.**7
   and single people in the housing market **85.**7
   statistics **40.**2
   young people's views on **40.**8
doctors
   and abortion
      case studies **71.**30, 31, 32, 33
      decision-making **71.**17
      law **71.**13, 18, 19, 37
      moral objections to **71.**1, 13, 18, 19, 29, 37, 39
      referrals **71.**1, 13
      and women's mental health **71.**34, 35, 36, 37
   and cancer **60.**6, 7, 32, 38
   cancer specialists (oncologists) **60.**14, 31, 36
   and combination therapy for HIV **10.**31
   and complementary medicine **81.**4
   and complementary therapies **60.**39

consultants **60**.31
and euthanasia **4**.4, 6-7, 18
and late abortions in Scotland **71**.38
and pain control **4**.16
and patients under 16 years **71**.39
and sports drug abuse **59**.27, 32
domestic violence **44**.1-40; **83**.6
and alcohol abuse **44**.4-5
causes of **44**.18
and child abuse **44**.4, 15-16, 28
and child marriages **65**.18
and children **44**.4, 5, 28, 29-33
costs of **44**.3, 13
defining **44**.4, 18, 29
different forms of **44**.4, 26
effects of **44**.19
government policies on **44**.8, 13, 23
impact of **44**.12-13
and the law
and children **44**.30
court injunctions **44**.23, 25, 27
current legislation **44**.8-9
and low self-esteem **66**.3
men as victims of **44**.6, 8, 20-1
mental or psychological abuse **44**.3, 34
myths about **44**.4-5
and the police **44**.3, 7-8, 10, 22-3, 24, 25, 26, 27
and rehousing **44**.37-8
seeking help **44**.26-40
survivors of **44**.12
truth about **44**.17
in the United States **44**.34
victims' accounts of **44**.20-1, 24-5
as a world-wide problem **44**.2, 34
and young women **44**.18-19
drug abuse **62**.1-17
and adolescent health **70**.6, 7, 8, 14-16
awareness and knowledge of drugs **70**.15-16
and early sex **70**.10
and anxiety **32**.6
and begging **83**.6

and bullying **73**.7
cannabis *see* cannabis
as a cause of stress **68**.2
and children of lone parents **75**.29
and children and young people in prison **83**.23
and the classification of drugs **80**.24
and 'cold turkey' **62**.6
and depression **68**.4, 8
drugs identification guide **62**.2
drugs seized by customs and the police **62**.3
education programmes on **62**.36
and employed young adults **62**.1-2
in Europe **62**.7-8
and girls in prison **83**.27, 28
Government drug strategy **62**.10, 15-17, 28, 38, 39
and gun crime **83**.4
and HIV infection **10**.14, 21, 29, 33
and homeless persons **79**.2, 10, 15
ex-servicemen **79**.21
young runaways **79**.29
and low self-esteem **66**.6, 20
and mental illness **84**.18
and missing persons **79**.13
patterns of **62**.4, 6, 14
and physical activity in young people **61**.3
physical effects of **62**.2, 5, 12
and prisoners **83**.8, 26
public attitudes to **80**.27-8
risk reduction **62**.13-14
in schools **62**.4-5, 9; **83**.12
and self-harm **77**.10, 24, 26
and social problems **62**.37
statistics on **80**.2
and stress **32**.18
and suicide **70**.36; **77**.3, 4, 18, 23
and teenage sex **75**.18
treatment services **62**.16, 17, 36
in the UK **62**.4-5, 14, 20
warning signs of **62**.2, 5-6
and young people *see* young people, and drug abuse
young people's attitudes to crime and **83**.17
drug testing **62**.19; **80**.2

Volume numbers appear first (in bold) followed by page numbers; a change in volume number is preceded by a semi-colon.

Vol. **3** The Animal Rights Debate
Vol. **4** The Euthanasia Issue
Vol. **10** Sexually Transmitted Diseases
Vol. **11** Fertility Rights
Vol. **16** Our Ageing World
Vol. **19** Looking at Vegetarianism
Vol. **20** Population Growth
Vol. **22** Confronting Child Abuse
Vol. **23** Sexuality
Vol. **25** The Changing Workplace
Vol. **27** The Censorship Issue
Vol. **28** The Global Warming Debate
Vol. **29** Gambling
Vol. **31** The Impact of the Internet
Vol. **32** Coping with Stress
Vol. **33** The Tourism Issue
Vol. **35** The Education Crisis?
Vol. **39** Alcohol Abuse
Vol. **40** The Future of Marriage
Vol. **43** A Consumer Society

Vol. **44** Confronting Domestic Violence
Vol. **46** Child Labour
Vol. **54** The Energy Debate
Vol. **55** Globalisation
Vol. **56** The Wealth Divide
Vol. **57** Waste Pollution
Vol. **58** The Transport Issue
Vol. **59** Issues in Sport
Vol. **60** Confronting Cancer
Vol. **61** Fitness
Vol. **62** Drugs and the Law
Vol. **63** The Racism Debate
Vol. **64** The Gender Issue
Vol. **65** Human Rights
Vol. **66** Self-Esteem
Vol. **67** Parenting
Vol. **68** Coping with Depression
Vol. **69** The Media
Vol. **70** Adolescent Health
Vol. **71** Abortion

Vol. **72** Obesity and Eating Disorders
Vol. **73** Dealing with Bullies
Vol. **74** Money Matters
Vol. **75** Lone-Parent Families
Vol. **76** The Water Crisis
Vol. **77** Self-inflicted Violence
Vol. **78** Threatened Species
Vol. **79** Dealing with Homelessness
Vol. **80** The Cannabis Debate
Vol. **81** Alternative Therapies
Vol. **82** Protecting our Privacy
Vol. **83** Dealing with Crime
Vol. **84** Mental Wellbeing
Vol. **85** The Housing Crisis
Vol. **86** Smoking and your Health
Vol. **87** Genetic Modification
Vol. **88** Food and Nutrition
Vol. **89** Refugees
Vol. **90** Human and Animal Cloning
Vol. **91** Disability Issues

drug treatments for depression **68**.13, 27
    manic depression **68**.33, 34
    seasonal affective disorder **68**.21
    side effects of **68**.27
drugs
    anabolic steroids *see* anabolic agents
    animal testing of **3**.3, 8, 13
    for anxiety and phobias **32**.7
    attitudes to illegal **43**.4
    and children's rights **65**.2, 5
    depression caused by **68**.19
    for female infertility **11**.3-4, 6, 8, 9, 27
    human clinical trials of **3**.11
    obesity **72**.5
    safety and animal experiments **3**.6, 12, 13, 15, 17
    for stress **32**.17
    withdrawn from the market **3**.11, 13, 15
drugs and the law **62**.18-39
    arguments for legalisation **62**.32-3, 37, 38-9
    arrest referral **62**.15
    classifications of drugs **62**.2, 3, 18, 19, 21, 26
    criminal records and employment **62**.19
    and driving **62**.19, 22
    effective drug policy **62**.36-7
    international law **62**.34
    main offences **62**.18
    making or growing your own **62**.18-19
    prosecution and punishment **62**.19, 22, 26
    protecting civil rights **62**.37
    public opinion on **62**.20
    reducing drug related crime **62**.36
    reducing drug related ill health **62**.36
    rights on arrest **62**.14, 19, 25
    travelling abroad **62**.19
    and treatment **62**.15
drugs in sport **59**.20-39
    amphetamines **59**.28
    athletics **59**.31, 33-4, 36, 37-8
    beta-blockers **59**.20, 29
    blood doping **59**.29
    and caffeine **59**.29
    cocaine **59**.28, 39
    diuretics **59**.20, 22, 29
    doping classes **59**.20
    doping methods **59**.20-1
    football **59**.25-6, 35, 39
    human growth hormones (hGHs) **59**.27, 28
    inadvertent doping **59**.34
    and the International Olympic Committee **59**.20-1
    and the media **59**.33-4
    medication and prohibited substances **59**.29, 34
    morphine **59**.28
    narcotic analgesics **59**.20, 21-2
    peptide hormones and analogues **59**.20, 22
    questions and answers **59**.29
    reasons for prohibiting **59**.36
    recreational drugs **59**.26, 35, 36, 39
    rugby league **59**.31
    signs and symptoms of drug use **59**.36
    stimulants **59**.20, 21
    testing

    athletes **59**.37-8
    blood tests **59**.21, 26
    footballers **59**.26, 35

E

e-mail
    access to **31**.2
    addresses and safety **31**.30, 33
    and computer viruses **31**.13
    decline in popularity of **31**.17
    educational uses **31**.8
    employer monitoring **31**.13, 14-15
    filtering **31**.18
    surveillance of
        and the Government **82**.1, 22, 23
        in the workplace **82**.25, 26, 27, 28, 30
    in the workplace **31**.13-18
eating disorders **61**.15; **67**.17; **72**.15-30; **84**.9, 21
    and adolescent health **70**.4, 34-6
    association with specific occupations **72**.20, 21
    binge-eating disorder **72**.16, 23
    and body image **72**.32, 37
    and body weight **72**.22
    causes of **72**.17
    and childhood **84**.29
    and children **72**.34
    compulsive overeating **72**.2, 9, 16, 17, 23
    danger signs **72**.14
    deaths from **72**.23
    eating 'normally' around others **72**.23
    health consequences of **72**.23
    helping friends with **72**.27
    and low calorie intake **72**.22
    and low self-esteem **66**.6, 10-13, 20, 25, 31
    and men **72**.16, 20, 21, 30
    overcoming **72**.17
    and perfectionism in teenage girls **70**.33
    and physical or sexual abuse **72**.17, 20
    prevention **72**.26, 30
    questions of carers and families about **72**.28-9
    risks of developing **72**.20
    teenagers and dieting **72**.13
    therapy **72**.29
    types of people suffering from **72**.22
    and vitamin supplements **72**.23
    women and extreme eating disorders **72**.24-5
eco-systems
    degradation of freshwater **76**.35
    and the extinction of bird species **78**.8
    and water consumption **76**.2, 16-17, 19
economy and refugees **89**.21, 22, 30-1
ecotourism **33**.15-17, 30-1
Ecstasy
    deaths from **80**.10, 11
    depression triggered by **68**.8
    employed young adults **62**.1
    and the law
        classification **62**.2, 18
        reclassification **62**.20

physical effects of **62**.2
prevalence of use **62**.4, 20
quantity seized in the UK **62**.3
signs of **62**.2
education **35**.1-40
  and basic skills of prisoners **83**.8
  and black pupils **35**.12-13
  and child labour
    effectiveness of **46**.18
    and government policies **46**.3
    parents' attitudes to **46**.1
  and children's rights **65**.5, 23
  common values and purposes of **35**.2
  in developing countries **20**.20, 28; **56**.21, 26, 30, 31,
      32, 39
  and disabled people **91**.7, 10, 29-36
  and ethnic minorities in the UK **63**.7
  examination performance **35**.7-11, 12, 17
  and gender *see* gender and education
  housing education **79**.12
  and the Human Rights Act **65**.25
  international development targets **55**.21
  and the Internet **31**.8-10
  jargon **35**.4-5
  and literacy levels **35**.5
  in mental health **84**.4, 30-2
  in money matters **74**.1, 5-6, 12, 13
  and older people **16**.6
  parenting classes **67**.22-3
  personal, social and health education **35**.1
  qualifications of refugees **89**.34-5
  and the Race Relations Act **63**.27-8
  and racism **63**.11-12
  school leavers and qualifications **35**.3-4
  science education **35**.6, 7
  and teenage parents **75**.1, 2
  and the Universal Declaration of Human Rights **65**.30
elderly people
  and beanpole families **67**.5
  and cancer **60**.3, 7, 14
  and dementia **84**.11, 12
  and euthanasia **4**.6

grandparents **67**.4, 14-15, 17, 33
growth in numbers of **20**.9, 11
and homelessness **79**.9
and housing **85**.2, 10, 15
living with their adult children **67**.4
and living wills **4**.40
and mental health problems **84**.1
older parents **67**.36-7
oldest old people **16**.1, 4, 9
and physical activity **61**.2, 10-11
and poverty
    in the developing world **56**.33
    in former socialist regimes **56**.24
    in the UK **56**.3, 14, 15
and television, complaints about programmes **69**.4
employers
  and child labour **46**.1, 4
  and childcare **25**.36
  costs of absenteeism **25**.5, 14
  and family-friendly working practices **64**.35
  and flexible working **25**.1
  overcoming sex stereotyping **64**.37
  and the pay gap **64**.24-5, 27, 28
  and privacy rights in the workplace **82**.25-30
  responsibilities and workplace bullying **73**.26, 31, 37
  and stress management **32**.14, 18, 19, 21, 27
employment
  in Britain today **25**.1, 2, 13
  and criminal records for drugs offences **62**.19
  of disabled people **91**.3, 4, 7, 10, 15-16, 19-20, 32
  employee assistance programmes **32**.26
  and ethnic minority groups **63**.9, 17, 38
  'flexible' labour policies and trade liberalisation **55**.29
  forecasts **25**.1
  gay rights in the workplace **23**.32-5
  and globalisation **55**.21, 37
  and lone parents **75**.30, 38
  and older people **16**.1, 3, 5, 8, 11, 13, 16-19, 24
  and pensions **16**.25-7
  and population growth **20**.6, 8
  self-employment and older workers **16**.13, 23
  and staff turnover **25**.5, 22

Volume numbers appear first (in bold) followed by page numbers; a change in volume number is preceded by a semi-colon.

Vol. 3   The Animal Rights Debate
Vol. 4   The Euthanasia Issue
Vol. 10 Sexually Transmitted Diseases
Vol. 11 Fertility Rights
Vol. 16 Our Ageing World
Vol. 19 Looking at Vegetarianism
Vol. 20 Population Growth
Vol. 22 Confronting Child Abuse
Vol. 23 Sexuality
Vol. 25 The Changing Workplace
Vol. 27 The Censorship Issue
Vol. 28 The Global Warming Debate
Vol. 29 Gambling
Vol. 31 The Impact of the Internet
Vol. 32 Coping with Stress
Vol. 33 The Tourism Issue
Vol. 35 The Education Crisis?
Vol. 39 Alcohol Abuse
Vol. 40 The Future of Marriage
Vol. 43 A Consumer Society

Vol. 44 Confronting Domestic Violence
Vol. 46 Child Labour
Vol. 54 The Energy Debate
Vol. 55 Globalisation
Vol. 56 The Wealth Divide
Vol. 57 Waste Pollution
Vol. 58 The Transport Issue
Vol. 59 Issues in Sport
Vol. 60 Confronting Cancer
Vol. 61 Fitness
Vol. 62 Drugs and the Law
Vol. 63 The Racism Debate
Vol. 64 The Gender Issue
Vol. 65 Human Rights
Vol. 66 Self-Esteem
Vol. 67 Parenting
Vol. 68 Coping with Depression
Vol. 69 The Media
Vol. 70 Adolescent Health
Vol. 71 Abortion

Vol. 72 Obesity and Eating Disorders
Vol. 73 Dealing with Bullies
Vol. 74 Money Matters
Vol. 75 Lone-Parent Families
Vol. 76 The Water Crisis
Vol. 77 Self-inflicted Violence
Vol. 78 Threatened Species
Vol. 79 Dealing with Homelessness
Vol. 80 The Cannabis Debate
Vol. 81 Alternative Therapies
Vol. 82 Protecting our Privacy
Vol. 83 Dealing with Crime
Vol. 84 Mental Wellbeing
Vol. 85 The Housing Crisis
Vol. 86 Smoking and your Health
Vol. 87 Genetic Modification
Vol. 88 Food and Nutrition
Vol. 89 Refugees
Vol. 90 Human and Animal Cloning
Vol. 91 Disability Issues

and students **74.**20, 29, 37
and teenage parents **75.**2
in tourism **20.**18
and training of employees **35.**4
in urban areas in the developing world **20.**18, 19-20
and young workers **25.**17-23
employment and racism **63.**5, 31
black workers and pay **63.**19-20
employment of refugees **89.**22-3, 24, 26-7, 32
illegal employment of refugees **89.**10-11, 30-1
language barriers **89.**27, 35, 37
pay rates **89.**22
permission to work documents **89.**35
qualifications of refugees **89.**34-5
right to work **89.**32, 34
seasonal labour **89.**22-3
endangered species **78.**1-3
birds **78.**2, 8-9, 27, 29, 37
in Britain **78.**28-31
and Chinese medicine **81.**15
and cloning **90.**21, 30
defining the term **78.**28
and the killing of wildlife **78.**2, 4-5, 5-6
mammals **78.**3, 27, 28, 32
plants **78.**2-3, 7, 17, 21, 36
and pollution **78.**6
primates **78.**3, 26
reptiles **78.**2
and responsible tourism **33.**27, 28
sharks **78.**15
trade in **78.**16-17, 19-22, 38-9
trees **78.**12
in the UK **78.**28-31
and urban development **78.**6
energy
calory intake **88.**1, 12
and food labelling **88.**21, 22
energy consumption **87.**24, 25
of electrical appliances **54.**34-5
fuel crisis in the UK **28.**37
and population growth **20.**6, 14
statistics **54.**2, 4, 6
in the UK **54.**3
energy efficiency **28.**27, 30, 33, 34, 36; **54.**2, 28-40
and consumer choice **54.**28, 29-31
developing technologies for **28.**37
and electrical appliances **54.**30, 32-3, 34-5
in the future **54.**40
and glass recycling **57.**29
government policies on **54.**35-6
in the home **54.**33, 35, 36
and incinerated waste **57.**6, 17, 19-20, 37
and sustainable housing **85.**37
environment
and animal experiments **3.**8
and globalisation **55.**7, 11, 16
and housing **85.**14-15, 26
and oil production **55.**29-30
and population growth **20.**1, 4, 8, 22-4
protection and children's rights **65.**23
and tourism **33.**4, 10-11, 17, 21, 29, 37

and trade liberalisation **55.**29
and vegetarianism **19.**6-7, 26, 27, 33
and water bills **76.**33, 34
equal pay **64.**17-22, 24-8
ethical trade **55.**4, 32
and slave labour **46.**11
ethnic minorities **63.**6-7
and adolescent health **70.**4, 6
and attitudes to advertising **69.**14
and aviation security **82.**3
and child poverty in London **85.**10
children's rights **65.**1, 4
in clubs and associations **63.**30
and the criminal justice system **63.**17-18, 33
defining ethnicity **63.**4
and educational achievement **35.**12
gender and education **64.**3, 8, 9
gender and work **64.**13
health **63.**7
history of in the UK **63.**2, 35
and homelessness **79.**10, 19
and identity cards **82.**2, 8
and Internet access **69.**3
and the labour market **63.**6-7
lifestyle **63.**7
mixed race population in the UK **63.**3
and multiculturalism **63.**2
numbers of older people in the UK **16.**1, 3
obesity in young women **72.**1, 2
and physical activity **61.**5
and poverty **56.**3, 14, 17
public attitudes to **63.**5, 8, 10
and sexual ill health **10.**2
size of UK population **63.**6
and soap operas **69.**8
and state benefits **63.**7
statistics **63.**6-7; **67.**6
and teenage parenthood **70.**12; **75.**2, 23
on TV and radio **63.**9
and the UK 2001 census **63.**3, 7
as victims of crime **63.**4, 7, 14-15, 17
euthanasia **4.**1-40
active **4.**1, 2, 4, 8
benefits and burdens **4.**19
and best interest **4.**19
and brain stem death **4.**9, 19
and cancer **4.**4, 12, 15-16, 18-19, 32
and capacity **4.**19
case against **4.**3, 8
and case law **4.**19
and changed attitudes to dying **4.**31
clear and constitutional law **4.**20
clear and convincing evidence **4.**19-20
and death from dehydration **4.**35
defining **4.**1, 2, 5, 10, 20
and difficult cases **4.**30
and the 'double effect' **4.**1, 4, 16, 20
and the fear of dying **4.**31
and guardian ad litem **4.**20
history of **4.**5
and individual autonomy **4.**7, 8, 18-19

and individual people **4**.30
involuntary **4**.1, 2, 3, 6
legislation in different countries **4**.14, 18
and life-sustaining treatments **4**.20
medical debate on **4**.22-32
medical power of attorney **4**.20
and palliative care **4**.3, 4, 8, 9, 12, 16, 21
passive **4**.1, 2, 4, 8
public attitudes to **4**.22
relatives assisting the terminally ill **4**.14, 15-16
religious views on **4**.2, 3, 6, 10
and resuscitation policies **4**.36-8
and the right to die with dignity **4**.17
and the right to life **4**.1, 5, 8
and the risk of abuse **4**.31
safeguards **4**.2
and substituted judgement **4**.21
and surrogate decision-making laws **4**.21
and terminal cancer **4**.4, 12, 15-16, 18-19, 32
and the treatment of the dying **4**.5-6, 15-16, 19, 30-1
versus good medical practice **4**.8
voluntary **4**.1, 2
withholding or withdrawing treatment **4**.21
exam stress **32**.2, 3-5
coping with exam results **32**.4
do's and don'ts **32**.3
and girls **70**.31-2
revision tips **32**.5
stress-busting tips **32**.5
and suicide **32**.9
exercise **61**.19-29, 38-9; **88**.1, 2-3, 11, 12, 18
active leisure activities **61**.32
activity in daily life **61**.32
aerobic exercise **61**.4, 20, 21
age and sex differences in **61**.2, 4
benefits of **58**.2, 5, 21; **61**.19, 21, 21-2, 26-8, 38
breathing exercises **32**.31, 36-7, 40
compulsive **72**.23
controlling stress through **32**.20, 25, 31, 32-3, 37, 38
cooling down **61**.23
costs of **61**.10
cycling **61**.1, 2, 8, 24

dancing **61**.24
decline in the UK **61**.4
defining **61**.8
and emotional health and wellbeing **84**.24, 27
ethnic differences in **61**.5
excuses for not exercising **61**.20
fitness fanatics **61**.38-40
health and physical benefits **16**.31; **61**.19, 26, 27, 28
and the heart **61**.21, 22, 28
jogging/running **61**.24
and life expectancy **61**.39
low-cost ways to exercise **61**.24
mental and psychological benefits **61**.19, 27, 28
motivation **61**.27
myths about **61**.10-11
and obesity **61**.8-9, 26
and older people **61**.2, 10-11
overall levels of **61**.4
and personal trainers **61**.25
physical activity referral schemes **72**.14
resistance training **61**.20
safety tips **61**.20
and self-esteem **66**.26, 28
social and economic benefits **61**.26, 27
socio-economic differences in **61**.4-5
time spent on **61**.2, 10, 21, 22
tips for becoming more active **61**.20
tips for staying active **61**.29
trampetting **61**.24
types of activity **61**.20, 22
videos **61**.24
walking **61**.1, 2, 8, 10, 24, 29, 32
warming up **61**.23
and weight **61**.8-9
and young people **61**.1-4, 6-7, 10, 23-4, 26; **70**.5, 24
extinction **20**.6, 8-9, 14, 21, 22; **78**.1-2
bird species at risk of **78**.8, 9, 27
increase in the rate of **78**.1-2, 10-11
and the killing of animals **78**.2, 4, 6
measuring rates of **78**.27
tree species at risk of **78**.12
and urban development **78**.6

Volume numbers appear first (in bold) followed by page numbers; a change in volume number is preceded by a semi-colon.

Vol. 3   The Animal Rights Debate
Vol. 4   The Euthanasia Issue
Vol. 10 Sexually Transmitted Diseases
Vol. 11 Fertility Rights
Vol. 16 Our Ageing World
Vol. 19 Looking at Vegetarianism
Vol. 20 Population Growth
Vol. 22 Confronting Child Abuse
Vol. 23 Sexuality
Vol. 25 The Changing Workplace
Vol. 27 The Censorship Issue
Vol. 28 The Global Warming Debate
Vol. 29 Gambling
Vol. 31 The Impact of the Internet
Vol. 32 Coping with Stress
Vol. 33 The Tourism Issue
Vol. 35 The Education Crisis?
Vol. 39 Alcohol Abuse
Vol. 40 The Future of Marriage
Vol. 43 A Consumer Society

Vol. 44 Confronting Domestic Violence
Vol. 46 Child Labour
Vol. 54 The Energy Debate
Vol. 55 Globalisation
Vol. 56 The Wealth Divide
Vol. 57 Waste Pollution
Vol. 58 The Transport Issue
Vol. 59 Issues in Sport
Vol. 60 Confronting Cancer
Vol. 61 Fitness
Vol. 62 Drugs and the Law
Vol. 63 The Racism Debate
Vol. 64 The Gender Issue
Vol. 65 Human Rights
Vol. 66 Self-Esteem
Vol. 67 Parenting
Vol. 68 Coping with Depression
Vol. 69 The Media
Vol. 70 Adolescent Health
Vol. 71 Abortion

Vol. 72 Obesity and Eating Disorders
Vol. 73 Dealing with Bullies
Vol. 74 Money Matters
Vol. 75 Lone-Parent Families
Vol. 76 The Water Crisis
Vol. 77 Self-inflicted Violence
Vol. 78 Threatened Species
Vol. 79 Dealing with Homelessness
Vol. 80 The Cannabis Debate
Vol. 81 Alternative Therapies
Vol. 82 Protecting our Privacy
Vol. 83 Dealing with Crime
Vol. 84 Mental Wellbeing
Vol. 85 The Housing Crisis
Vol. 86 Smoking and your Health
Vol. 87 Genetic Modification
Vol. 88 Food and Nutrition
Vol. 89 Refugees
Vol. 90 Human and Animal Cloning
Vol. 91 Disability Issues

eyes
    retinoblastomas **60**.9, 11
    and UV exposure **60**.19, 20

F

factory farming **19**.24, 30-1, 35-6, 37-8
    and agricultural experiments on animals **3**.8
    and animal suffering **19**.38
fair trade **55**.4
    and ecotourism **33**.22, 25
    products **55**.30, 32, 38
    and slave labour **46**.11
    ways to encourage fairer trade **55**.30
families **67**.1-16
    and abortion **71**.32
    and adolescent health **70**.6, 7, 8
    British attitudes to parents with young children **67**.7
    changes in after divorce **40**.30-2
    changing family patterns **67**.2, 18
    changing trends in family life **40**.1-4
    and child labour **46**.3
    and child trafficking **46**.20
    of compulsive gamblers **29**.28
    costs of family breakdown **67**.10
    and crime prevention **83**.36
    and debt problems **74**.3, 5-6
    diversity of family forms **67**.1
    family backgrounds of homeless people **79**.18
    and fertility issues **11**.26-7
    and gay couples **23**.36-7
    grandparents **67**.4, 14-15, 17, 33
    homeless **79**.4, 11, 19, 33
    and homophobia **23**.18, 19
    and the Human Rights Act **65**.24-5
    lone parents and successful family life **67**.39
    and mental illness **84**.8-10
    of prisoners **83**.39
    and self-esteem **66**.1-2, 12-13
    sitting down to meals together **67**.2
    and soap operas **69**.8-9
    and the spending power of tweenagers **74**.4
    and suicide **70**.36; **77**.33, 36-8
    and teenage parenthood **75**.2
    telling about HIV-positive status **10**.29-30
    of vegans **19**.11, 12
    of vegetarians **19**.11
    and violence **44**.19
    weekly family conferences **67**.22
family planning **20**.11, 25-40
    and the education of girls **20**.3, 9
    funding **20**.30
    humanist views on **11**.26-7
    international conferences and programmes **20**.21, 25-6, 28, 36-8, 39-40
    and maternal mortality **20**.25, 28, 29, 30
    and population growth **20**.3, 10
    and reproductive rights **20**.27-8, 35
    and sexual health **20**.27, 28, 33-5, 39-40
    stabilizing population through **20**.24

farmers
    and animal welfare **19**.35-6
    and the anti-milk campaign **19**.17
    cloning farm animals **90**.30, 39
    and illegal hare coursing **3**.37
fast foods
    backlash against **61**.35, 36
    and the cannabis economy **80**.8
    consumer market for **43**.10
    and dieting **72**.38
    and litter **57**.11, 12, 21
    and obesity **61**.7; **72**.6, 33-4
    and teenagers **43**.6, 7
    see also junk food
fat intake **88**.2, 5, 7, 8
    in the diet **61**.30-1, 34, 37
    and food labelling **88**.21-2, 22-3
    lower fat food choices **61**.33
    and obesity in girls and young women **72**.2
    reducing **19**.10
    vegan diets **19**.14
fathers **67**.11, 24-31
    and abortion **71**.25, 37
    absent, and suicidal young men **77**.33
    advice for **67**.27
    attitudes to **67**.25
    and authoritative parenting **67**.29
    and boys' reading **64**.2
    as breadwinners **67**.11
    characteristics of young fathers **70**.12
    child murders by **44**.8, 30
    and childcare **67**.25, 30-1
    and children's self-esteem **66**.39
    cohabiting **67**.29
    common complaints against **67**.26
    of disabled children **67**.26
    and the family **67**.29
    first-time **67**.27-8
    and girls' perfectionism **70**.32
    and lifestyle changes **67**.28
    living apart from children **67**.26, 28, 29
    lone fathers **75**.28, 34-6
    and long working hours **67**.39
    married **67**.11, 29
    paternity leave **25**.24, 25, 29, 33; **56**.16; **64**.11, 17, 33, 34, 35
    rights of, and abortion **71**.25, 37
    separated
        and debt **75**.37
        relationships with children **75**.36
    stay-at-home **67**.25, 30-1, 35
    stepfathers **67**.13, 27, 28
    time spent in the kitchen **67**.2
    unmarried fathers and parental responsibility **40**.14; **65**.11
    working fathers **64**.34-5
    young fathers
        and paid paternity leave **75**.12
        and parental responsibility **75**.12
        socio-economic background **75**.1, 2
        support for **75**.8

fear of crime **83**.6, 38
feminism
    case for abortion **71**.18
    and censorship **27**.31-2
fertility ethics **11**.26-40
fertility laws **11**.10
fertility rates *see* birth rates
fertility rights **11**.10, 38, 39
fertility treatment **11**.6, 11-17; **90**.11
fibre crops **87**.20
fibre intake **88**.2, 5, 6, 23
film censorship **27**.1-8
flexible working **25**.1, 25, 28-9, 32
floods **28**.9, 10, 12, 15, 23, 26
food
    and animal cloning **90**.39
    children and **43**.7
    energy efficiency **54**.30
    energy intake **70**.25-6
    expenditure on **43**.1, 3, 13
    fair trade products **55**.30
    flavours in tobacco **86**.7
    growth of market in **43**.10
    hunger and malnutrition **56**.1, 22, 24-5
    and older people in the developing world **56**.33
    and population growth **20**.2-3, 6, 8, 13, 24
    production and climate change **28**.13, 26
    production and global water supplies **76**.3, 4, 7, 18
    and schizophrenia **84**.14-15
    supplies in developing countries **20**.18, 24
    taxes on unhealthy foods **61**.7, 9
    weekly expenditure on **56**.1, 12
food labelling **87**.3-4, 5, 6, 9, 11, 13, 32; **88**.9, 21-5
    additives **88**.34
    consumer attitudes to **88**.26
    defrosting and cooking times **88**.23
    health claims **88**.21-2, 30
    and healthy diets **61**.30
    legislation **88**.23, 24, 25
    nutrition information panels **88**.21, 22-3
    storage instructions **88**.23
    understanding **61**.37

    use by dates **88**.23
    and value for money **88**.22
food and nutrition **88**.1-39
    additives **88**.13-14, 34, 36, 38, 39
    and adolescent health **70**.6, 25-6
    advertising and promotion **88**.10, 11, 19, 20, 35, 37
    consumer attitudes **88**.26, 36-7
    food poisoning **88**.14, 27-9
    food quality **88**.13-14
    food safety **88**.26, 32, 34
    and fruitarian diets **19**.1
    healthy diet **88**.1-2, 5-7
    junk food **88**.9-11
    and macrobiotic diets **19**.1
    nutrition information panels **88**.21, 22-3
    policing the food supply chain **88**.38
    portion sizes **88**.1, 5, 17
    regular eating **88**.1, 8
    supplements **88**.7
food poisoning **88**.14, 27-9
    and animal products **19**.3, 7, 16
football
    and child labour **46**.16
    drug abuse in **59**.25-6, 35, 39
    racism in **59**.1-11
football hooliganism **59**.11, 12-19
    arrest figures **59**.14, 19
    and banning orders **59**.12, 14, 15-16, 19
    decline in **59**.17, 19
    increase in **59**.13
    legislation **59**.15, 18
    and points penalties **59**.12
    and the police **59**.11, 12, 13, 14-17
    and self-policing by fans **59**.10
football pools
    age restrictions **29**.18, 27
    expenditure on **29**.9
    and men **29**.8, 9
    online **29**.12
    percentage of the population participating **29**.7
forests
    carbon 'sinks' **28**.16, 20, 27

Volume numbers appear first (in bold) followed by page numbers; a change in volume number is preceded by a semi-colon.

Vol. **3**   The Animal Rights Debate
Vol. **4**   The Euthanasia Issue
Vol. **10** Sexually Transmitted Diseases
Vol. **11** Fertility Rights
Vol. **16** Our Ageing World
Vol. **19** Looking at Vegetarianism
Vol. **20** Population Growth
Vol. **22** Confronting Child Abuse
Vol. **23** Sexuality
Vol. **25** The Changing Workplace
Vol. **27** The Censorship Issue
Vol. **28** The Global Warming Debate
Vol. **29** Gambling
Vol. **31** The Impact of the Internet
Vol. **32** Coping with Stress
Vol. **33** The Tourism Issue
Vol. **35** The Education Crisis?
Vol. **39** Alcohol Abuse
Vol. **40** The Future of Marriage
Vol. **43** A Consumer Society

Vol. **44** Confronting Domestic Violence
Vol. **46** Child Labour
Vol. **54** The Energy Debate
Vol. **55** Globalisation
Vol. **56** The Wealth Divide
Vol. **57** Waste Pollution
Vol. **58** The Transport Issue
Vol. **59** Issues in Sport
Vol. **60** Confronting Cancer
Vol. **61** Fitness
Vol. **62** Drugs and the Law
Vol. **63** The Racism Debate
Vol. **64** The Gender Issue
Vol. **65** Human Rights
Vol. **66** Self-Esteem
Vol. **67** Parenting
Vol. **68** Coping with Depression
Vol. **69** The Media
Vol. **70** Adolescent Health
Vol. **71** Abortion

Vol. **72** Obesity and Eating Disorders
Vol. **73** Dealing with Bullies
Vol. **74** Money Matters
Vol. **75** Lone-Parent Families
Vol. **76** The Water Crisis
Vol. **77** Self-inflicted Violence
Vol. **78** Threatened Species
Vol. **79** Dealing with Homelessness
Vol. **80** The Cannabis Debate
Vol. **81** Alternative Therapies
Vol. **82** Protecting our Privacy
Vol. **83** Dealing with Crime
Vol. **84** Mental Wellbeing
Vol. **85** The Housing Crisis
Vol. **86** Smoking and your Health
Vol. **87** Genetic Modification
Vol. **88** Food and Nutrition
Vol. **89** Refugees
Vol. **90** Human and Animal Cloning
Vol. **91** Disability Issues

conservation and endangered birds **78**.2
deforestation **28**.8, 9, 10, 11; **78**.11
and global warming **28**.3, 8, 18, 30
fossil fuels **54**.1, 2-3; **87**.24
burning **28**.1, 7; **54**.4, 5, 11, 12, 14
and cars **58**.1, 5, 33
compared with wind energy **54**.15
cuts in emissions **28**.38-9
geographical changes in supply of **54**.19
and global warming **28**.4, 8, 10, 11, 25, 28, 29; **54**.7
importance of **54**.7, 38
non-renewability of **54**.1, 2-3, 7
phasing out of **54**.10, 28
vested interests of companies **54**.5
fostering
and adoption **71**.10
and duty of care **65**.11
foxes and foxhunting **3**.24-5, 26, 27, 28-36
fraud **43**.26-7
credit card **31**.37-8, 39, 40; **43**.26-7
and identity cards **82**.2, 7, 8, 11, 12
preventing **43**.34-7
fraud on the Internet **43**.26, 28, 39-40
auction fraud **31**.39, 40
credit card fraud **31**.37-8, 39, 40; **43**.26-7
domain name games **31**.40
preventing **43**.35, 37
scams **31**.39-40
stock market **31**.40
free trade
in agriculture **88**.33
and the anti-globalisation movement **55**.12-13
and child trafficking **46**.13
defining **55**.3-4
and developing countries **55**.32
loss of support for **55**.40
see also trade liberalisation
freedom of information **65**.39
fruit and vegetables **61**.30, 32, 34; **88**.2, 4, 5, 9, 12, 17, 26, 31
and children **61**.36
consumption by young people **70**.25
further education **91**.35
colleges **35**.19-21, 22
and gender **64**.8

G

gambling **29**.1-40
age restrictions on **29**.27
amount of money placed on a bet **29**.3
bingo **29**.2, 3, 7, 8, 9, 18, 22, 27
bookmaker bets **29**.7, 9, 12
expenditure on **29**.8-9, 17
football pools **29**.3, 7, 8, 9, 12, 18, 27
fruit machines **29**.1, 2, 7, 8, 9, 35, 36, 40
horse racing **29**.2, 3, 7, 8, 9, 19
international comparisons **29**.1-2, 7, 9
libertarian arguments for **29**.23
minimal interest gamblers **29**.8, 9

multiple interest gamblers **29**.8, 9
odds of winning **29**.2
percentage of non-gamblers **29**.7-8
problem gamblers **29**.35
reasons for present law **29**.1
responsible **29**.38
systems **29**.28
UK law on
liberalisation **29**.1, 16, 17, 18-19, 22-3
online gambling **29**.12
and women **29**.3, 8, 9, 26
and young people **29**.2, 37-8
and plastic cash **43**.24
see also casinos; compulsive gambling; National Lottery
gas, natural gas **54**.3, 7
gay couples
and adoption **23**.38
children of **23**.37, 40; **67**.16
compensation for deaths as a result of crime **23**.37
and fertility rights **11**.27, 38, 40
marriages **40**.18
reproduction and human cloning **90**.21
rights of **23**.30, 36-7
gay men
age of consent for gay sex **23**.17, 19, 29-30, 39, 40
Catholic priests **23**.22-3
and condom use **10**.2
and criminal convictions for sexual offences **23**.34
and eating disorders **72**.21
feeling about sexuality **23**.7, 25, 29
and fertility laws **11**.10
and HIV infection **10**.14, 27, 29, 32-3
numbers of **23**.25
and promiscuity **23**.15, 25
public attitudes to **23**.16
and sex discrimination in the workplace **23**.34
and sexually transmitted infections **10**.5
and soap operas **69**.8-9
use of the term gay **23**.1, 2
workplace discrimination **23**.32-5
see also homosexuality
gender
and attitudes to advertising **69**.14
and debt problems **43**.30
and drug misuse in the UK **62**.4, 5, 20, 27
equality and suicidal feelings in young men **77**.33
income disparities **56**.15
and Internet access **31**.1
lone parents and changing gender relations **75**.31
and mental health problems **84**.1
and participation in gambling **29**.3, 8, 9
theory of AIDS/HIV **10**.25
and young offenders **83**.15
and young people's attitudes to crime **83**.16
see also men; women
gender and education **64**.1-9
and examination results **64**.4, 5, 6, 7, 8, 9
further education and vocational training **64**.8
and the gender pay gap **64**.25
girls and information technology (IT) **64**.14
higher education **64**.8-9

and science subjects **64**.14
in Scotland **64**.7, 9
statistics **64**.3
and subject choices **64**.7
and young women in Europe **64**.3
gender relationships **64**.33-9
and household financial decision-making **64**.36
and sex stereotyping **64**.37
work and family life **64**.33-5
gender and work **64**.10-32
and equal pay **64**.17-22
global inequalities **64**.1
and occupation **64**.10, 11-12, 13, 19, 21, 25-6, 28, 37
and skills gaps **64**.37
and the UK labour market **64**.13
working fathers **64**.34-5
and young women in Europe **64**.10-11
genes **87**.1-2
altering **87**.2
controlling gene expression **87**.22
gene pharming **90**.29-30, 32, 35
and homosexuality **23**.7, 25, 26
inserting **87**.2, 17, 22
and male infertility **11**.1
switching off **87**.2, 20; **90**.2
therapy **90**.11
transfer from GM food to body cells **87**.8, 17, 33
genetic engineering **90**.21
genetically modified (GM) crops **19**.7; **88**.14, 32, 33
allergenicity of GM crops **87**.8, 17, 18, 19-20
Britain and GM crops **87**.14-16
commercial crop growing **87**.10, 31
consumer attitudes to **87**.3-4, 5-7, 16
cross-contamination **87**.18, 20, 21, 30, 31-2
field trials **87**.10, 11
legal battles **87**.32
legislation **87**.6, 10-11, 30
non-food crops **87**.20, 37-8
profitability from GM crops **87**.15, 31
public opinion **87**.3-4, 5-7, 16
safety controls **87**.6, 8, 9, 17, 30, 39
testing procedures **87**.10, 17, 18

girls and young women
alcohol abuse **39**.5; **70**.7, 24
and body image **72**.34
and bullying **35**.13
cannabis effects on mental health **62**.8; **68**.7
and child abuse **22**.12, 13
as child soldiers **46**.10, 28, 35, 37, 38, 39
and depression **68**.1, 4, 9
in developing countries **20**.25, 34
and dieting **72**.2, 13, 35
and domestic violence **44**.18-19
as domestic workers **46**.3, 4, 10
and drug abuse **70**.14
and eating disorders **70**.35; **72**.15-19, 20, 22-30, 35
and education **25**.30, 31
and exercise **61**.2, 4; **70**.24
and expenditure on the National Lottery **29**.35
and gender inequality **64**.1, 2
and information technology (IT) **64**.14
life expectancy **70**.8
and obesity **72**.1-3, 6
and perfectionism **70**.31-3
and pocket money **64**.13
prison custody and under 18s **83**.23, 27-9
rates of disability **91**.4
and school bullying **73**.5-7
schoolchildren working illegally **25**.20
and self-harm **70**.37; **77**.6-7, 20, 24
sexual abuse and exploitation **40**.25; **46**.19, 25-6
sexual behaviour **20**.26, 34; **70**.10, 13; **75**.17, 18, 19
and sexually transmitted infections **70**.4
and smoking **70**.7, 17, 18
and suicide **32**.8; **77**.2, 5
and vegetarian diets **19**.1
and waist measurement **70**.27
and work **64**.10-11
glacial melting **28**.10, 15, 17-18, 19-20, 26, 30, 40
glass recycling **57**.4, 5, 21, 22
centres **57**.28, 30
energy saved by **57**.29
process of **57**.28
re-use of ground glass **57**.18

Volume numbers appear first (in bold) followed by page numbers; a change in volume number is preceded by a semi-colon.

Vol. 3   The Animal Rights Debate
Vol. 4   The Euthanasia Issue
Vol. 10 Sexually Transmitted Diseases
Vol. 11 Fertility Rights
Vol. 16 Our Ageing World
Vol. 19 Looking at Vegetarianism
Vol. 20 Population Growth
Vol. 22 Confronting Child Abuse
Vol. 23 Sexuality
Vol. 25 The Changing Workplace
Vol. 27 The Censorship Issue
Vol. 28 The Global Warming Debate
Vol. 29 Gambling
Vol. 31 The Impact of the Internet
Vol. 32 Coping with Stress
Vol. 33 The Tourism Issue
Vol. 35 The Education Crisis?
Vol. 39 Alcohol Abuse
Vol. 40 The Future of Marriage
Vol. 43 A Consumer Society

Vol. 44 Confronting Domestic Violence
Vol. 46 Child Labour
Vol. 54 The Energy Debate
Vol. 55 Globalisation
Vol. 56 The Wealth Divide
Vol. 57 Waste Pollution
Vol. 58 The Transport Issue
Vol. 59 Issues in Sport
Vol. 60 Confronting Cancer
Vol. 61 Fitness
Vol. 62 Drugs and the Law
Vol. 63 The Racism Debate
Vol. 64 The Gender Issue
Vol. 65 Human Rights
Vol. 66 Self-Esteem
Vol. 67 Parenting
Vol. 68 Coping with Depression
Vol. 69 The Media
Vol. 70 Adolescent Health
Vol. 71 Abortion

Vol. 72 Obesity and Eating Disorders
Vol. 73 Dealing with Bullies
Vol. 74 Money Matters
Vol. 75 Lone-Parent Families
Vol. 76 The Water Crisis
Vol. 77 Self-inflicted Violence
Vol. 78 Threatened Species
Vol. 79 Dealing with Homelessness
Vol. 80 The Cannabis Debate
Vol. 81 Alternative Therapies
Vol. 82 Protecting our Privacy
Vol. 83 Dealing with Crime
Vol. 84 Mental Wellbeing
Vol. 85 The Housing Crisis
Vol. 86 Smoking and your Health
Vol. 87 Genetic Modification
Vol. 88 Food and Nutrition
Vol. 89 Refugees
Vol. 90 Human and Animal Cloning
Vol. 91 Disability Issues

returnable bottles **57.**22, 29
statistics **57.**29
global democracy **55.**23-4
global warming **28.**1-40; **54.**2, 5, 7, 14, 28
and cars **58.**1, 5
causes of **28.**8
and clouds **28.**3, 10, 39
and deforestation **28.**8, 9, 10, 11
and developing countries **28.**27, 39
effects of **28.**7-28, 40
and food supplies **28.**13, 26
and fossil fuel burning **28.**4, 8, 10, 11, 25, 28, 29; **54.**7
and glacial melting **28.**10, 15, 17-18, 19-20, 26, 30, 40
government policies on **28.**36, 37, 38, 40
and ice cover thawing **28.**4, 10-11, 15, 18-20
and the 'ice-albedo' effect **28.**3
and livestock cultivation **19.**6
and local climate change **28.**4, 10, 11
and nuclear energy **54.**7
and pollution **28.**3, 13, 23-4, 25-7, 39
and population growth **20.**23, 24
and sea level rises **28.**7, 9, 10-11, 15, 16, 17, 18, 26
and sea temperature measurements **28.**21
solutions to **28.**29-40
and the Sun **28.**39
and water supplies **28.**19-20, 26
and water vapour **28.**3
and wildlife **28.**20, 23-4, 30, 35
globalisation **43.**10-11; **55.**1-40
alternatives to **55.**39-40
anti-globalisation views **55.**2, 7, 12-13, 39-40
and children **55.**1-2, 34
and consumerism **43.**10-11
criticisms of **55.**8-10, 16
debate on **55.**7-40
defining **55.**2-3, 14, 20, 35
and economic change **55.**1-2
and global trade **55.**9-10
origins of **55.**3
and poverty **55.**1-2, 15, 20-2, 27, 35-9; **56.**21, 26
supporters of **55.**40
and trade liberalisation **55.**29
and workers' rights **55.**11, 26
gonorrhoea **10.**1, 2, 3, 5, 6-7
rates in the UK **10.**11
symptoms **10.**6-7
tests for **10.**7
treatment **10.**7
graduates
pay gap **64.**25
recruiting disabled graduates **91.**19-20
starting salaries **74.**31
unemployment and ethnic minorities **63.**11
women **64.**9, 13, 14
and work-life balance **25.**15
grandparents **25.**37; **40.**31, 38; **67.**14-15, 17
and childcare **67.**4, 33
greenfield sites
house-building on **85.**9, 25
guidelines on **85.**28
and housing density **85.**34

in the M11 region **85.**18
in the Thames Gateway **85.**23, 24
and urban renewal **85.**35
greenhouse effect **28.**2, 7, 29
and cars **58.**1
and pollution **28.**23-4, 25
and scientists **28.**3
and temperature rises **28.**8-9
greenhouse gas emissions **20.**23, 24; **28.**1, 14; **54.**2, 4-7, 9
atmospheric levels of **28.**17
and developing countries **28.**27
and forests **28.**3
and global temperature rises **28.**1, 15, 17, 20-3, 25, 31
levels **28.**2-3, 5, 17
and nuclear power **54.**7, 8
and ocean currents **28.**3
reducing **28.**5, 6, 16, 27, 31-6, 40
and the UK government **54.**6-7, 11, 14, 35
timeline from 1827 to the present **28.**5-6
in the UK **28.**33, 34, 36, 37
in the USA **28.**6
gun crime **83.**3, 4, 18

H

habitat loss
and endangered wildlife in Britain **78.**30-1, 32
and Globally Threatened Birds **78.**8, 9
and otters **78.**33
and species extinction **78.**10
hallucinogens
and the law, classification **62.**3, 18
physical effects of **62.**3
signs of **62.**3
harassment
as a criminal offence **23.**35
of lesbian and gay employees **23.**35
and work-related stress **32.**13, 14
and workplace bullying **73.**36-7
Government policies on **73.**37
health
and ageing **16.**5, 28-40
and alcohol **39.**2-3, 5, 7, 9-10, 15-16, 25-8, 26, 35, 37
and animal experiments **3.**17
and animal products **19.**16
and beggars **79.**34, 35
benefits of optimism **66.**15
and cannabis **80.**7, 10, 12, 13, 15
and child labour **46.**1, 10
and children's rights **65.**2, 4-5, 23
of cloned animals **90.**27, 28, 31, 34, 39
of cloned humans **90.**1, 2, 3, 7, 9
damage caused by traffic pollution **58.**5, 15
and diet **61.**13, 30
and domestic violence **44.**2, 19, 27, 31
effects on children travelling by car **58.**21
expenditure on health and fitness **43.**1
health consequences of being bullied **73.**2, 6-7, 29
and homeless people **79.**15
and marriage **40.**7, 10

medical treatment of older people **16**.6
and obesity **61**.6, 12, 37, 38; **70**.30; **72**.1, 8-9, 10, 12, 37
and physical activity **61**.10-11, 19, 26, 27
and poverty **56**.1, 2, 22, 30, 31
and smoking **70**.18-19
and stress **32**.11, 16, 20, 22, 24, 33
and surrogate mothers **11**.24
and teenage pregnancy and parenthood **75**.1, 2
and vegetarian diets **19**.15, 20, 26, 33
and walking **58**.2, 5
health care
    age discrimination in **16**.11, 28, 35
    children's rights and parental responsibility **65**.12
    in developing countries **20**.18
    and disabled people **91**.11, 37-8, 39
    international development targets **55**.21
    in poor countries **55**.38
    and refugees **89**.19-20
health and safety at work
    and tourism **33**.4
    and work-related stress **32**.18
    and young workers **25**.18
healthy eating **88**.1-2, 5-7
    balanced diets **61**.29-31, 33, 34, 37
    and dieting **72**.38
    and meat consumption **19**.4-5, 8, 10
    and vegan diets **19**.12
    and vegetarian diets **19**.7, 9, 20
    see also food and nutrition
heart disease
    and alcohol consumption **39**.37
    and aromatherapy **81**.10
    and complementary therapies **81**.21
    and diet **61**.13
    and eating disorders **72**.37
    and meat consumption **19**.4, 15
    and milk consumption **19**.17, 18
    and obesity **61**.15; **72**.6, 7, 8-9, 37
        in children **61**.6; **72**.4, 5
        in women **72**.1
    and physical activity **61**.4-5, 20, 26, 27
    in Scotland **61**.11

and smoking **86**.2, 3, 9-11, 13, 24-5, 31
and stress **32**.20, 34, 35-6
and vegetarians **19**.7, 8, 16, 19, 20
hedgerows **87**.15
    decline of in Britain **78**.30
    and foxhunting **3**.38-9
herbal medicine **81**.4, 11, 23, 36
    banned herbs **81**.24
    Chinese **81**.14-15
    choosing a reputable practitioner **81**.23-4
    defining **81**.2, 11
    and depression **68**.12, 37
    effectiveness of **81**.24
    expenditure on **81**.37
    medical conditions treated by **81**.11
    and multiple sclerosis **81**.30
    Natural Medicines Society HerbAlert campaign **81**.38
    and pharmaceutical drugs **81**.11
    regulation of **81**.23
    risks of **81**.24
    and scientists **81**.28, 29
herbicides **87**.1, 7, 9, 10, 23, 24, 25, 29, 32
heroin
    and drug misuse in Europe **62**.7
    and the law
        classification **62**.3, 18
        new guidelines on prescribing **62**.20, 39
        treatment services **62**.16
    and opium production in Afghanistan **62**.38
    physical effects of **62**.3
    prescriptions **62**.20, 39
    quantity seized in the UK **62**.3
    school pupils and prevalence of use **62**.4, 5, 9
    signs of **62**.3
heterosexuality
    assumptions of **23**.3
    defining **23**.2
    and gay lifestyles **23**.6
    and HIV infections **10**.1-2, 14, 20, 21, 29, 35
    and homophobia **23**.19-20
    stereotypes of **23**.3
high blood pressure (hypertension) **19**.15; **72**.1; **88**.2, 9

Volume numbers appear first (in bold) followed by page numbers; a change in volume number is preceded by a semi-colon.

Vol. **3**   The Animal Rights Debate
Vol. **4**   The Euthanasia Issue
Vol. **10** Sexually Transmitted Diseases
Vol. **11** Fertility Rights
Vol. **16** Our Ageing World
Vol. **19** Looking at Vegetarianism
Vol. **20** Population Growth
Vol. **22** Confronting Child Abuse
Vol. **23** Sexuality
Vol. **25** The Changing Workplace
Vol. **27** The Censorship Issue
Vol. **28** The Global Warming Debate
Vol. **29** Gambling
Vol. **31** The Impact of the Internet
Vol. **32** Coping with Stress
Vol. **33** The Tourism Issue
Vol. **35** The Education Crisis?
Vol. **39** Alcohol Abuse
Vol. **40** The Future of Marriage
Vol. **43** A Consumer Society

Vol. **44** Confronting Domestic Violence
Vol. **46** Child Labour
Vol. **54** The Energy Debate
Vol. **55** Globalisation
Vol. **56** The Wealth Divide
Vol. **57** Waste Pollution
Vol. **58** The Transport Issue
Vol. **59** Issues in Sport
Vol. **60** Confronting Cancer
Vol. **61** Fitness
Vol. **62** Drugs and the Law
Vol. **63** The Racism Debate
Vol. **64** The Gender Issue
Vol. **65** Human Rights
Vol. **66** Self-Esteem
Vol. **67** Parenting
Vol. **68** Coping with Depression
Vol. **69** The Media
Vol. **70** Adolescent Health
Vol. **71** Abortion

Vol. **72** Obesity and Eating Disorders
Vol. **73** Dealing with Bullies
Vol. **74** Money Matters
Vol. **75** Lone-Parent Families
Vol. **76** The Water Crisis
Vol. **77** Self-inflicted Violence
Vol. **78** Threatened Species
Vol. **79** Dealing with Homelessness
Vol. **80** The Cannabis Debate
Vol. **81** Alternative Therapies
Vol. **82** Protecting our Privacy
Vol. **83** Dealing with Crime
Vol. **84** Mental Wellbeing
Vol. **85** The Housing Crisis
Vol. **86** Smoking and your Health
Vol. **87** Genetic Modification
Vol. **88** Food and Nutrition
Vol. **89** Refugees
Vol. **90** Human and Animal Cloning
Vol. **91** Disability Issues

HIV (human immunodeficiency virus) 10.1-2, 14-40
    and adolescents 70.9
    average survival age 10.17
    bodily fluids containing 10.18, 21
    and child marriages 65.18
    children with 10.2
    and children's rights 65.15, 16, 23
    in developing countries 20.18, 20, 33
        Africa 10.15, 16-17, 26-7; 56.22, 27
        Asia 10.15, 17, 27, 34
        China 10.35
        Eastern Europe 10.14, 17
        Russia 10.17
    and development aid 56.35
    diagnosis 10.22
    and drug abuse 10.14, 17, 21-2, 29, 33
    groups at risk of 10.21
    and heterosexual sex 10.1-2, 14, 20, 21, 29, 36
    HIV-positive
        and healthy living 10.32
        living with HIV 10.28-30
        pregnant women 10.15, 16, 22, 30
        support groups 10.27
        telling partners, friends and families 10.29-30
    and homosexual sex 10.2, 14, 20, 21
    human costs of 10.2
    and infected needles 10.19
    means of transmission 10.19, 21-2
    and normal social contact 10.19, 29
    numbers of infections 10.15, 16
        in sub-Saharan Africa 10.16-17
        in the UK 10.1, 2, 3, 14, 20
        worldwide 10.37
        and young people 10.23, 32
    and population growth 20.5
    prevention programmes 20.25, 27, 28, 30, 37
    projects for children 64.2
    questions and answers 10.18-20
    and 'seroconversion' illness 10.26
    and sex education 75.21, 22, 24
    and sexual behaviour 75.16
    statistics 20.36, 39
    symptoms of infection 10.20, 22, 26, 31
    testing asylum seekers 89.20
    tests 10.12, 19-20, 31-2
    types of virus 10.21
    vaccine development 10.39-40
    worldwide prevention programmes 10.32-3, 36-7, 38
    worldwide statistics 10.16-17, 22, 27
    and young people 10.23; 20.34
holidays
    and British workers 25.13, 17
    expenditure on 43.1
        cruises 43.3
        long-haul destinations 43.4
    and the over 50s 16.9-10
    seaside holidays and responsible tourism 33.26
    see also package holidays; responsible tourism
home ownership
    and consumer spending 43.8
    and debt-stress 43.30

house price inflation 43.4, 8
    and people in their 50s 16.8
home-based working 25.8-9, 10, 11, 27
    see also teleworking
homeless households 79.4, 11, 19, 33; 85.11
    and London's housing problems 85.12, 13
    and the Sustainable Communities Plan 85.39
    in temporary accommodation 85.1, 3, 8, 11
homeless young people 79.4, 11, 20-1, 23-5
    and bed-and-breakfast accommodation 79.33-4
    emergency accommodation for 79.24
    fear of homelessness 79.22
    finding accommodation for 79.27
    and the Homelessness Act (2002) 79.33
    and the law 79.31
    and the police 79.28-9, 31
    reasons for homelessness 79.23
    risks faced by 79.23
    rough sleepers 79.22, 23
    runaways 79.23-4, 25, 28-9
    and the Safe in the City initiative 79.17, 28-9
    Shelter London case studies 79.36
    statistics 79.29
    street children in the UK 79.23-4
    and teenage parenthood 75.2
    under 16s 79.31
    and the withdrawal of benefits 79.35
homelessness
    and adolescent health 70.6, 7
    and affordable housing 79.1, 2, 9, 11-12, 35
    and beggars 79.26, 34-5
    and children 79.4, 8
    defining 79.10
    and domestic violence 44.10; 79.13, 37
    and drug misuse 62.9
    effects of 79.12
    and ex-servicemen 79.21
    Government policies on 79.3, 7
    and health 79.15, 39
    the 'hidden homeless' 79.10, 39
    and human rights 79.32
    and the law 79.8, 30
        Homelessness Act (2002) 79.2, 3, 8-9, 24, 33
        and young people 79.31
    and mental health problems 79.2, 10, 15, 16-17, 19
        beggars 79.34, 35
    and missing persons 79.13-14
    needs of homeless people 79.18
    and older people 79.9
    public attitudes to 79.4, 32
    reasons for 79.1, 2, 4, 10-11, 12, 18, 20-1
    registering as homeless 79.30
    research into 79.3, 5-7, 17, 39
    and the 'revolving door' syndrome 79.32, 33-4
    in Scotland 79.3, 10-12, 39
    and sexual abuse 46.25
    statistics 79.10, 19, 32, 36
    stereotypes of homeless people 79.20, 21
    tackling 79.27-39
    and teenage parenthood 70.12
    and 'throwaways' (institutionalized people) 79.1

homeopathy **81.**12-13, 23, 36
   and cancer **81.**32
   defining **81.**2, 12
   and diet **81.**13
   effectiveness of **81.**22, 24, 28
   expenditure on **81.**37
   and misdiagnosis **81.**24
   and the NHS **81.**4
   and the placebo effect **81.**26
   and scientists **81.**28-9
   treatments **81.**12-13
homicide
   and abortion **71.**14
   and guns **83.**4
   increase in rates of **83.**3
   racist **63.**13, 16
   victims of domestic violence **44.**2-3, 8, 10, 22, 35
homophobia **23.**17-20
   homophobic bullying **23.**18, 31, 40; **73.**6, 11
   and politics **23.**18-19
   and religion **23.**18
   and young people **23.**17-18
homosexuality
   and AIDS/HIV **10.**2, 14, 20, 21; **23.**12, 17, 24
   and Christianity **23.**5, 8, 12, 21, 24-6
   'coming out' **23.**3, 9-10
   'curing' **23.**5, 8, 20, 26
   defining **23.**2-3, 24
   feelings developing in adulthood **23.**7
   gay subculture **23.**24
   and genetics **23.**7, 25, 26
   and homophobia **23.**17-20
   legal aspects of **23.**5, 29-40
      age of consent **23.**17, 19, 29-30, 39, 40
      employment protection **23.**32-5
      and judges **23.**36-7
      rights of gay couples **23.**30, 36-7
   and lifestyle **23.**3, 6
   and marriage **23.**3, 5, 36-7
      gay marriages **23.**15, 19, 30, 38
   nature of **23.**3-4
   negative images of **23.**13

objections to **23.**12-13
positive images of **23.**13-14
and prejudice **23.**3-4, 14, 16, 17-18
psycho-social explanations of **23.**8, 18, 20, 25-6
and sex education **23.**10-12, 13-14, 18
statistics on **23.**36
stereotypes of **23.**3
terminology **23.**1, 2
and young people **23.**5, 7, 8, 10-12, 13-14, 19; **70.**13
   prejudice among **23.**17-18
horse racing
   age restrictions on gambling **29.**2
   expenditure on **29.**9
   future of **29.**19
   and interactive television **29.**19
   and men **29.**8
   percentage of people participating **29.**7
   and women **29.**3
hospice movement **60.**8, 13
   and euthanasia **4.**3, 4, 12, 15-16, 20, 25
hospitality industry **86.**17, 19, 20-3
hospitals
   admissions and young people **70.**3-4, 6
   and cases of self-harm **77.**6, 9, 10, 29
      changing A & E staff attitudes to **77.**26
   and mental illness **84.**10, 36
      and the draft mental health bill **84.**36-7
hostels **79.**32-4
hotels
   and civil marriages **40.**5
   and responsible tourism **33.**13, 26, 28, 40
hours of work
   children working illegal hours **25.**20
   'desk rage' **32.**26, 30
   effects on children **32.**10
   increase in **43.**3
   long hours culture **25.**4; **32.**14, 15, 27, 28
   and lunch hours **32.**30
   night workers **25.**17, 29
   and stress management **32.**32-3
   working fathers **64.**34
   working mothers **67.**18, 19, 32, 33, 39

Volume numbers appear first (in bold) followed by page numbers; a change in volume number is preceded by a semi-colon.

Vol. 3   The Animal Rights Debate
Vol. 4   The Euthanasia Issue
Vol. 10 Sexually Transmitted Diseases
Vol. 11 Fertility Rights
Vol. 16 Our Ageing World
Vol. 19 Looking at Vegetarianism
Vol. 20 Population Growth
Vol. 22 Confronting Child Abuse
Vol. 23 Sexuality
Vol. 25 The Changing Workplace
Vol. 27 The Censorship Issue
Vol. 28 The Global Warming Debate
Vol. 29 Gambling
Vol. 31 The Impact of the Internet
Vol. 32 Coping with Stress
Vol. 33 The Tourism Issue
Vol. 35 The Education Crisis?
Vol. 39 Alcohol Abuse
Vol. 40 The Future of Marriage
Vol. 43 A Consumer Society

Vol. 44 Confronting Domestic Violence
Vol. 46 Child Labour
Vol. 54 The Energy Debate
Vol. 55 Globalisation
Vol. 56 The Wealth Divide
Vol. 57 Waste Pollution
Vol. 58 The Transport Issue
Vol. 59 Issues in Sport
Vol. 60 Confronting Cancer
Vol. 61 Fitness
Vol. 62 Drugs and the Law
Vol. 63 The Racism Debate
Vol. 64 The Gender Issue
Vol. 65 Human Rights
Vol. 66 Self-Esteem
Vol. 67 Parenting
Vol. 68 Coping with Depression
Vol. 69 The Media
Vol. 70 Adolescent Health
Vol. 71 Abortion

Vol. 72 Obesity and Eating Disorders
Vol. 73 Dealing with Bullies
Vol. 74 Money Matters
Vol. 75 Lone-Parent Families
Vol. 76 The Water Crisis
Vol. 77 Self-inflicted Violence
Vol. 78 Threatened Species
Vol. 79 Dealing with Homelessness
Vol. 80 The Cannabis Debate
Vol. 81 Alternative Therapies
Vol. 82 Protecting our Privacy
Vol. 83 Dealing with Crime
Vol. 84 Mental Wellbeing
Vol. 85 The Housing Crisis
Vol. 86 Smoking and your Health
Vol. 87 Genetic Modification
Vol. 88 Food and Nutrition
Vol. 89 Refugees
Vol. 90 Human and Animal Cloning
Vol. 91 Disability Issues

young managers **25.**23
young workers **25.**17
house prices **85.**1, 3-4
house-building
    affordable housing, and homelessness **79.**1, 2, 9, 11-12, 35
    properties built on flood plains **28.**28
household waste
    alternatives to disposable items **57.**20-1
    amounts of **57.**2, 3, 15, 17
    charging for the disposal of **57.**17, 18, 39
    clothing **57.**36
    composition of **57.**1, 2
    and the Ecoteam programme **57.**38
    and energy production **57.**37
    and the EU landfill directive **57.**1
    Government policies on **57.**14, 15, 16, 17, 20, 29, 39
    kerbside collections of **57.**17, 18, 24
    and packaging **57.**15, 20, 22, 25
    recycling **57.**4, 5, 16, 17, 20, 21, 22-3
    tips regarding **57.**20-1, 25
    see also composting waste; waste management
households
    average size of **43.**2
    expenditure patterns **43.**1, 2, 3-4
        gap between rich and poor **43.**13; **56.**12
    financial decision-making within **64.**36
    growth in numbers of **85.**1-2, 3, 29
        and the need for new homes **85.**8-9, 20
    incomes and financial decisions **56.**15
    low income **56.**3, 4
    number of single-person **75.**29
    size in the UK **67.**2
    weekly expenditure **43.**13
housework
    sharing responsibility for **25.**16
    time spent doing **25.**25
    time spent in **67.**2
    and working mothers **67.**35
housing
    age of houses in the UK **85.**30
    bed-and-breakfast accommodation **79.**33-4
    costs **79.**9
    and domestic violence
        hostels for abusive men **44.**38-9
        rehousing victims of **44.**37-8
    and the environment **85.**14-15, 26
    expenditure on **79.**9
    home ownership in the UK **85.**30
    housing crisis 'backlog' **85.**2
    in London **85.**10-13, 16-17
    and lone parents **75.**38
    need for new homes **85.**1-3, 8-9
    and 'neighbourhood collapse' **85.**38
    new house-building
        on brownfield sites **85.**9, 26, 34, 35
        and Building for Life **85.**36
        in cities **85.**25
        and housing density **85.**25, 34
        in the M11 region **85.**18, 22, 26, 27, 33
        numbers being built **85.**3

        and planning permission **85.**35
        in the Thames Gateway **85.**21-4, 26, 33
    numbers of empty houses **79.**9
    numbers of new homes being built **85.**3
    and overcrowded accommodation **79.**1
    poverty and poor housing conditions **79.**9
    and the Race Relations Act **63.**28
    size of houses in the UK **85.**30
    and teenage mothers **70.**12
    and teenage parenthood **75.**2
    unsaleable houses **43.**4
    and urban growth in developing countries **20.**17-18
housing associations
    and house-building **85.**24
    in London
        and shared ownership houses **85.**11
        and unfit dwellings **85.**12
    and private developers **85.**19
human reproductive cloning **90.**1-25
    arguments against **90.**1, 24
    arguments for **90.**1, 3-4
    autonomy issues **90.**4
    bans on **90.**10, 11, 14, 22, 25, 33
    behavioral similarities to donors **90.**8, 12, 20
    biological age **90.**9
    conflicts of interest **90.**4
    and a conscious brain **90.**20
    definition of a clone **90.**2
    and dignity **90.**4, 5
    ethical standards **90.**3, 4, 12, 15, 18, 19, 22
    familial relations **90.**9
    and gay couple reproduction **90.**21
    and gene therapy **90.**11
    health of cloned humans **90.**1, 2, 3, 7, 9
    identity of cloned humans **90.**8
    and infertility treatments **90.**11
    licences for embryo research **90.**23
    miscarriage risks **90.**7
    mixing human cells and animal eggs **90.**19
    and motherhood **90.**8-9
    research milestones **90.**21
    and super-human people **90.**20-1
    uses for **90.**3
human rights **65.**24-39
    and CCTV **82.**24
    and censorship on the Internet **27.**10, 11
    and child protection **22.**25-6
    and children's rights **65.**1-23
    and fertility rights **11.**10, 38-40
    and film censorship **27.**5
    and freedom of information **65.**38-9
    and homelessness **79.**32
    legislation **65.**71
    and privacy rights **82.**4-5, 18
    and responsible tourism **33.**24, 25
    and school bullying **73.**11, 17-18
    and terrorism **65.**31-2
    water as a human right **76.**24-5, 32
    and women's rights **65.**33
humanists
    and abortion **71.**3, 15, 17-18

and animal welfare **3**.1, 2
and fertility issues **11**.26-7
hunting
for bushmeat **78**.18
and mammals in the UK **78**.32
welfare of horses **3**.28
whales **78**.6, 13, 14
of wildlife **78**.2, 4-5, 5-6
hydroelectric energy **54**.1, 3, 13, 36
and dams **57**.23
power stations **57**.23
small-scale schemes (SHPs) **54**.11, 12, 13
in the UK **54**.7, 8, 13

identical people **90**.1, 2, 3, 20
identity of cloned humans **90**.8
identity (ID) cards **82**.1, 2, 7-12
and biometric data **82**.9, 10, 12
and bogus asylum seekers **82**.7, 8
built into passports and driving licenses **82**.9-10, 12
and civil liberties **82**.11-12
and communities **82**.11
and electronic fraud **82**.11
fee to be charged for **82**.7, 8, 10
fraud **82**.7, 8
and health and welfare benefit abuse **82**.7, 8, 9
and identity fraud **82**.11, 12
and the National Identity Register **82**.9, 11, 12
opposition to **82**.7, 8
and personal freedom **82**.8
and plans for a national population computer database **82**.3
public attitudes to **82**.7-8
illegal immigrants **89**.11, 30-1
immigrants *see* asylum seekers; ethnic minorities
immigration
and population growth **20**.4-5, 11, 15-16, 32
and the UK population **67**.3
incomes

and the ageing population in the UK **16**.1-2
of black people **63**.19-20
Britain compared with European countries **25**.3
and debt problems **43**.30, 31
defining poverty by income **56**.1, 2, 7, 8
and educational qualifications **35**.3
gambling and income levels **29**.3, 8
and globalisation **55**.35
and house prices **85**.1, 3
in London **85**.10-11, 12
regional variations in **85**.3-4, 8
inequality of **43**.4, 13; **56**.1, 21
and gender **56**.15
global **56**.37
and lone parents **75**.31
low income households **56**.3, 4
national minimum wage **25**.17; **43**.4; **56**.13, 18; **64**.22; **75**.10
necessary for older people **16**.11
and the over 50s **16**.9, 10
of pensioners in different countries **16**.12
post-graduate **35**.32
and spending on leisure and tourism **33**.2
students and part-time jobs **35**.40
in workless households **16**.17
industry
water consumption **76**.2, 8, 36
water pollution **76**.11
weakness of British **43**.10
inequality and poverty **56**.1
and globalisation **55**.1-2, 6, 21, 23, 37
and household spending **56**.12
and trade liberalisation **55**.29, 36
see also child poverty; poverty
infant mortality **20**.28, 29, 30, 31; **56**.28, 35, 37
international targets for reducing **55**.21
and social class **56**.4
and teenage mothers **75**.2
infertility **11**.1-2, 5; **86**.25
and age **11**.5, 9, 11
blocked Fallopian tubes **11**.3, 4, 5, 6, 8
causes of **11**.1-2, 3, 5, 8

Volume numbers appear first (in bold) followed by page numbers; a change in volume number is preceded by a semi-colon.

Vol. 3   The Animal Rights Debate
Vol. 4   The Euthanasia Issue
Vol. 10 Sexually Transmitted Diseases
Vol. 11 Fertility Rights
Vol. 16 Our Ageing World
Vol. 19 Looking at Vegetarianism
Vol. 20 Population Growth
Vol. 22 Confronting Child Abuse
Vol. 23 Sexuality
Vol. 25 The Changing Workplace
Vol. 27 The Censorship Issue
Vol. 28 The Global Warming Debate
Vol. 29 Gambling
Vol. 31 The Impact of the Internet
Vol. 32 Coping with Stress
Vol. 33 The Tourism Issue
Vol. 35 The Education Crisis?
Vol. 39 Alcohol Abuse
Vol. 40 The Future of Marriage
Vol. 43 A Consumer Society

Vol. 44 Confronting Domestic Violence
Vol. 46 Child Labour
Vol. 54 The Energy Debate
Vol. 55 Globalisation
Vol. 56 The Wealth Divide
Vol. 57 Waste Pollution
Vol. 58 The Transport Issue
Vol. 59 Issues in Sport
Vol. 60 Confronting Cancer
Vol. 61 Fitness
Vol. 62 Drugs and the Law
Vol. 63 The Racism Debate
Vol. 64 The Gender Issue
Vol. 65 Human Rights
Vol. 66 Self-Esteem
Vol. 67 Parenting
Vol. 68 Coping with Depression
Vol. 69 The Media
Vol. 70 Adolescent Health
Vol. 71 Abortion

Vol. 72 Obesity and Eating Disorders
Vol. 73 Dealing with Bullies
Vol. 74 Money Matters
Vol. 75 Lone-Parent Families
Vol. 76 The Water Crisis
Vol. 77 Self-inflicted Violence
Vol. 78 Threatened Species
Vol. 79 Dealing with Homelessness
Vol. 80 The Cannabis Debate
Vol. 81 Alternative Therapies
Vol. 82 Protecting our Privacy
Vol. 83 Dealing with Crime
Vol. 84 Mental Wellbeing
Vol. 85 The Housing Crisis
Vol. 86 Smoking and your Health
Vol. 87 Genetic Modification
Vol. 88 Food and Nutrition
Vol. 89 Refugees
Vol. 90 Human and Animal Cloning
Vol. 91 Disability Issues

Christian views on **11.**28-9
and impotence **11.**1
organisations to contact for help **11.**2, 4
and sexually transmitted infections (STIs) **70.**11
tests **11.**2, 3, 8-9, 9, 28
see also IVF (in vitro fertilisation); surrogacy
information fatigue syndrome **31.**17-18
information technology (IT)
and the 'digital divide' **55.**36
girls and educational performance **64.**14
importance of skills **25.**2
women and careers in **64.**12, 13
insects **78.**1
insomnia **32.**31, 40
insurance
life insurance for vegetarians **19.**19
and privacy rights **82.**25-6
weather-related claims **28.**28
and young people **74.**2, 15
integrated medicine/healthcare **81.**36-8
intellectual property rights **87.**29, 32
intelligence, and animal rights **3.**3
intensive farming **88.**31-2
interest rates
and consumer spending **43.**1, 8
and credit **74.**23
credit card **43.**28; **74.**26, 27
and mortgage repayments **85.**6
and savings **74.**24
internally displaced persons **89.**1, 6, 8-9
international trade
and developing countries **55.**31-2, 33-4, 35-6
and oil **55.**29
rules of **55.**24-6, 40
and transnational corporations **55.**18, 27
unfair protectionist policies **55.**33
see also globalisation
Internet **31.**1-40
access **69.**1, 3
advertising for sperm donors **11.**7
and alcohol marketing to young people **39.**13, 14
banking **74.**2
banning children from using **22.**22
and British consumers **43.**10
broadband connections **31.**11, 12, 18
bullying by e-mail **73.**25
censorship **27.**1, 3, 9-13; **31.**34, 35
chatrooms **31.**8, 20, 20-4, 21, 22-3, 26, 29, 30
commercial websites **31.**27-8
correct Internet behaviour **31.**33
credit card security **31.**30-1, 37-8
domestic violence support groups **44.**34-5
and education **31.**8-10
fake/morphed/edited images **31.**28
family Internet code **31.**32-3
financial services **31.**3, 4
flaming **31.**33
fraud **43.**26, 28, 39-40
frequency of access **31.**2
and globalisation **55.**1, 11, 35
and holiday bookings **33.**9-10, 11, 12

household access **31.**1, 12; **40.**1; **43.**3
identifying 'family-friendly' Internet providers **22.**39
information on goods and services **31.**2
instant messaging **31.**3, 23, 24
mailing lists **31.**8
and marital breakups **40.**36
newsgroups **31.**8, 24, 34
and older people **16.**12, 17
online banking **31.**3-4
online bullying **73.**3
online gambling **29.**3, 4, 7, 10-15, 23
online monitoring of internet activity **82.**17
online shopping **31.**2, 4
and paedophiles **31.**22-3, 28, 29, 30, 31, 35-6
people who do not use **31.**2, 12
pornography **27.**11-13, 38; **31.**23-4, 27, 29, 31, 34-5
posting of the names of sex offenders **22.**32
and racism **31.**28-9
rate of adoption **31.**12
reasons for people not using **31.**2
safety **31.**19-40
in schools **27.**11-12; **31.**5, 8, 23-4
service providers, voluntary code of practice for **82.**2
spamming **31.**33, 39, 40
support groups for victims of domestic violence **44.**34
surveillance
and the Government **82.**1, 22, 23
in the workplace **82.**25, 26, 27, 28
and technologies of privacy **82.**5
video conferencing **31.**8
and work-life balance **25.**12
in the workplace **31.**13-15
iridology **81.**17-18
irrigation **87.**35
and global water supplies **76.**3, 4, 5, 19
and inefficient water use **76.**36
and water conservation **76.**27
and water shortages **76.**21
IVF (in vitro fertilisation) **11.**6, 9, 11, 12-13, 15-17, 28; **90.**12, 19
cost of treatment **11.**17
and discrimination **11.**32
and donor eggs and sperm **11.**13-14, 37-8
ethics of **11.**20-30, 26, 27, 29, 31, 35-6, 38, 39
and female infertility **11.**4
and fertility rights **11.**38
and frozen embryos **11.**17
and the HFEA **11.**10
and male infertility **11.**2
natural cycle **11.**16-17
and pre-implantation diagnosis (PID) **11.**29-30
stimulated cycle **11.**15-16
storage of extra embryos **11.**13
success rates **11.**4, 14, 15, 17
and surrogacy **11.**18, 19, 20

J

jobseekers and transport **58.**15
judiciary

and gay marriages **23**.38
  guidelines for on the treatment of homosexuals **23**.36
junk food **72**.38; **88**.9-11
  advertising **72**.11, 14, 34
  and eating disorders **72**.22
  see also fast foods; food and nutrition
junk mail **82**.36
juries, attitudes to domestic violence **44**.23

K

ketamine **62**.21
key workers
  affordable housing for **85**.1, 3, 20
    in the Thames Gateway **85**.21, 22, 23
    see also public sector workers
kidney cancer **60**.5, 16, 17
  in childhood **60**.9, 11
kinesiology **81**.2

L

labour market, and ethnic minorities in the UK **63**.6-7
land use planning *see* planning policies
landfill sites **57**.1, 15, 16, 19, 29
  and car tyres **57**.7-8
  clothes in **57**.35, 36
  EU landfill directive **57**.1, 6, 15, 17, 37, 39
  future of **57**.37
  and glass **57**.28
  methane emissions **57**.1, 3, 5, 15, 24
  old computers dumped in **57**.33
  and organic waste **57**.1
  and paper **57**.34
  problems for local communities **57**.3
  UK compared with other countries **57**.18
  and zero waste policies **57**.39
  see also waste management
language
  barriers to employment **89**.27, 35, 37

BBFC guidelines on **27**.20, 22, 30
inappropriate use of mental health labels **84**.2
strong language on television **27**.38-9
tests **89**.37
to describe disability **91**.6
law centres
  and consumer complaints **43**.23
  and debt problems **43**.34
leaflet distribution **69**.29
learning disabilities **91**.26-39
  and mental illness **84**.2
  verbal abuse of children with **73**.12-13
  young people with, and teenage pregnancies **75**.24
lesbians
  and egg-fusion **11**.31
  and fertility rights **11**.10, 38, 39
  and motherhood **67**.16
  public attitudes to **23**.16
  and school bullying **73**.6, 11
  and sex discrimination in the workplace **23**.35
  and soap operas **69**.8-9
  use of the term 'lesbian' **23**.1
  workplace discrimination **23**.32-5
  see also gay couples; homosexuality
leukaemia **60**.5, 9, 16, 17, 33
life expectancy
  and adolescent health **70**.8
  and AIDS **20**.3, 5, 11
  in developed regions **20**.5
  in the developing world **56**.37
  and fitness **61**.39
  gains in average **20**.20
  and gender **16**.30
  global **16**.4, 10
  and globalisation **55**.35
  and health crisis **16**.32-3
  of homeless people **79**.16
  increase in **85**.2
  increases in **16**.9, 15, 16, 29
  and infant deaths **16**.29
  in less developed regions **20**.5, 18
  narrowing gap between the sexes **43**.2

Volume numbers appear first (in bold) followed by page numbers; a change in volume number is preceded by a semi-colon.

Vol. **3** The Animal Rights Debate
Vol. **4** The Euthanasia Issue
Vol. **10** Sexually Transmitted Diseases
Vol. **11** Fertility Rights
Vol. **16** Our Ageing World
Vol. **19** Looking at Vegetarianism
Vol. **20** Population Growth
Vol. **22** Confronting Child Abuse
Vol. **23** Sexuality
Vol. **25** The Changing Workplace
Vol. **27** The Censorship Issue
Vol. **28** The Global Warming Debate
Vol. **29** Gambling
Vol. **31** The Impact of the Internet
Vol. **32** Coping with Stress
Vol. **33** The Tourism Issue
Vol. **35** The Education Crisis?
Vol. **39** Alcohol Abuse
Vol. **40** The Future of Marriage
Vol. **43** A Consumer Society

Vol. **44** Confronting Domestic Violence
Vol. **46** Child Labour
Vol. **54** The Energy Debate
Vol. **55** Globalisation
Vol. **56** The Wealth Divide
Vol. **57** Waste Pollution
Vol. **58** The Transport Issue
Vol. **59** Issues in Sport
Vol. **60** Confronting Cancer
Vol. **61** Fitness
Vol. **62** Drugs and the Law
Vol. **63** The Racism Debate
Vol. **64** The Gender Issue
Vol. **65** Human Rights
Vol. **66** Self-Esteem
Vol. **67** Parenting
Vol. **68** Coping with Depression
Vol. **69** The Media
Vol. **70** Adolescent Health
Vol. **71** Abortion

Vol. **72** Obesity and Eating Disorders
Vol. **73** Dealing with Bullies
Vol. **74** Money Matters
Vol. **75** Lone-Parent Families
Vol. **76** The Water Crisis
Vol. **77** Self-inflicted Violence
Vol. **78** Threatened Species
Vol. **79** Dealing with Homelessness
Vol. **80** The Cannabis Debate
Vol. **81** Alternative Therapies
Vol. **82** Protecting our Privacy
Vol. **83** Dealing with Crime
Vol. **84** Mental Wellbeing
Vol. **85** The Housing Crisis
Vol. **86** Smoking and your Health
Vol. **87** Genetic Modification
Vol. **88** Food and Nutrition
Vol. **89** Refugees
Vol. **90** Human and Animal Cloning
Vol. **91** Disability Issues

and pensionable age **16**.25, 26-7, 32
regional differences in **16**.6
and smoking **86**.31
in the UK **16**.6, 29
wealth inequalities in **16**.17
and women **16**.6, 7, 29-30, 32, 33
lifestyle
and adolescent health **70**.7, 9
and cuts in greenhouse gas emissions **28**.37
encouraging fairer trade through **55**.30
and health in old age **16**.30, 31
and homeopathy **81**.13
and integrated healthcare **81**.36
and naturopathy **81**.19
and obesity **61**.8; **72**.6
in children **72**.4, 11
in girls and young women **72**.2
older people and active lifestyles **61**.10-11
of people in their 50s **16**.8
promoting healthy lifestyles **72**.9
sedentary lifestyles
and children **61**.1, 2, 3, 8, 10
in developing countries **61**.11
and diet **61**.13
and sensible eating **61**.33
and sexuality **23**.3, 6
and the species extinction crisis **78**.11
literacy
in Britain **35**.5
and gender **64**.1
literature, and ethnic minorities in the UK **63**.2
litter **57**.9-13
causes of **57**.10
clearing up **57**.9, 10-11
dangers of **57**.9
and the law **57**.9, 10
marine litter **57**.13
and packaging **57**.10
plastic bags **57**.32
public attitudes to **57**.9
and rats **57**.11-12
liver cancer **10**.1; **60**.5, 9, 16, 17
livestock farming
and animal rights **3**.4
and the environment **19**.6-7, 26, 27
living alone
numbers of people **85**.2
older people **16**.2, 3
people in their 50s **16**.8
living standards
and children's rights **65**.5
in the developing world **56**.26, 28, 37
and increased life expectancy **16**.29
and the Universal Declaration of Human Rights **65**.30
and water consumption **76**.8
living wills **4**.1, 7, 9, 20, 33-40
advantages of making **4**.36
and the artificial prolongation of life **4**.34
British Medical Association (BMA) views on **4**.38
and comfort-only care **4**.40
dangers of binding directives **4**.33

defining **4**.36
defining our fears **4**.33
elderly people's views on **4**.40
and emergency medication **4**.38
and the expression of the wish to die **4**.34
how to make **4**.37
and the inability to communicate **4**.34
legal enforcement of **4**.36, 40
and the prevention of mistreatment in hospital **4**.35
problems of executing **4**.33-4
public attitudes to **4**.40
and PVS (persistent vegetative state) **4**.39
and 'quality of life' **4**.34-5
refusal to sign **4**.35
restrictions on **4**.33, 36-7
and resuscitation attempts **4**.37-8
and voluntary euthanasia **4**.36
local authorities
and child abuse **22**.5, 12
and globalisation **55**.39
and homelessness **79**.8
and mental health, positive steps to **84**.27
and speed management **58**.30-1
transport policies **58**.27, 28, 29, 30-1
and victims of domestic violence **79**.37
see also care leavers
lone parents **20**.26, 33; **75**.28-39
and the breakdown of cohabitation **40**.4, 9, 12-13
and changing gender relations **75**.31
and child tax credit (CTC) **56**.16
and childcare **75**.30, 38, 39
children of **40**.2, 24, 31, 39-40; **75**.28, 29
looking after **75**.39
and children's behaviour **39**.20
and the costs of family breakdown **67**.10
and daughters of teenage mothers **75**.2
and divorce **75**.28, 31, 33, 35
money matters **75**.38
and employment **75**.30
in full-time work **75**.37-8
starting work **75**.39
fathers **75**.28, 34-6
financial management **75**.37-8, 39
and Gingerbread **75**.33, 34, 37
and the Government's 'family-first' Budget (1997) **75**.37
and household income **75**.31
and housing **75**.38
images of **67**.1
looking to the future **75**.39
making your family work **67**.39
marital status **75**.28, 31, 32
myths about **75**.28, 32, 33
never-married **75**.28, 31, 32
numbers of **40**.1
and paedophiles **22**.28
and parenting classes **67**.23
and poverty **40**.2; **56**.17; **75**.31, 32, 39
and relationships with fathers **67**.25-6
responsibilities of **75**.33
in Scotland **75**.31

in soap operas **69**.8
and State benefits **75**.31, 38
statistics **40**.2; **75**.28, 29, 31, 32
and stress **32**.34
students **74**.39
and suicide of children **77**.38
teenage mothers **70**.12
in work **25**.25
low self-esteem (LSE)
and behaviour patterns **66**.6, 14, 20, 21, 29
children with **66**.2, 38
costs and causes of **66**.6
and eating disorders **66**.6, 10-13, 20, 25, 31; **72**.17, 23
and economic outcomes **66**.6
impact of **66**.3
and insecurity **66**.17-18
and obesity
in children **72**.4
in girls and young women **72**.3
symptoms of **66**.3
therapy for **66**.3, 7, 12
see also self-esteem
lung cancer **60**.3
and cannabis **62**.28, 35
deaths **60**.3, 15, 27
and passive smoking **60**.16, 17
in Scotland **61**.11
and smoking **60**.4, 13, 15; **86**.5, 6, 9-11, 14-16, 31
survival rates **60**.4, 6, 14
treatment **60**.4
lymphomas **60**.4, 9, 10, 33

M

malnutrition, and poverty **56**.1, 22, 24-5, 33
management style, and workplace bullying **73**.25, 39
managers
and long working hours **25**.2, 6
see also hours of work
and office rage **32**.26
salaries of male managers **64**.15, 16, 22, 23

travelling costs of 'Didcot manager' **25**.10
women **25**.16, 30, 32; **64**.11, 12, 15-16, 23, 24, 39
and the pay gap **64**.24
and work-life balance **25**.4
and work-related stress **32**.13, 14-15, 25
and workplace absence rates **25**.14
young **25**.22-3
marriage
advantages of **40**.3
age of **40**.1, 3, 5, 6, 13
arranged marriages **40**.21-2
attitudes of married couples **40**.11
births outside **67**.6
changing attitudes to **40**.3, 19-20, 40
children and experiences of unhappy marriages **40**.39
Christian views on **40**.3-4, 10, 19
civil marriages **40**.3, 5, 13, 15
decline of **40**.15
early and forced marriage **65**.18, 19, 20, 35
and extra-marital affairs **40**.7, 15
and fathers **67**.11, 29
and financial decision-making **74**.6
health benefits of **40**.7, 10
and homosexuality **23**.3, 5
and the Human Rights Act **65**.25
importance of for children **40**.3, 10
increased expectations of **40**.6
and the law **40**.14, 17-18, 19, 20
length of marriages ending in divorce **40**.18
marital breakups and the Internet **40**.36
and the millennium **40**.5, 13
number of marriages **40**.5, 16, 19, 20
and population growth **40**.5
rates **40**.3, 5, 6, 13, 40
reasons for marital conflict **40**.7
religious wedding ceremonies **40**.5, 13, 14, 15, 18, 20
remarriages **40**.1-3, 5-7, 19-20
in Scotland **40**.18
and sex education **23**.10
as slavery **65**.35
social pressures against **23**.25
statistics on **40**.2, 3, 5, 13

Volume numbers appear first (in bold) followed by page numbers; a change in volume number is preceded by a semi-colon.

Vol. 3   The Animal Rights Debate
Vol. 4   The Euthanasia Issue
Vol. 10 Sexually Transmitted Diseases
Vol. 11 Fertility Rights
Vol. 16 Our Ageing World
Vol. 19 Looking at Vegetarianism
Vol. 20 Population Growth
Vol. 22 Confronting Child Abuse
Vol. 23 Sexuality
Vol. 25 The Changing Workplace
Vol. 27 The Censorship Issue
Vol. 28 The Global Warming Debate
Vol. 29 Gambling
Vol. 31 The Impact of the Internet
Vol. 32 Coping with Stress
Vol. 33 The Tourism Issue
Vol. 35 The Education Crisis?
Vol. 39 Alcohol Abuse
Vol. 40 The Future of Marriage
Vol. 43 A Consumer Society

Vol. 44 Confronting Domestic Violence
Vol. 46 Child Labour
Vol. 54 The Energy Debate
Vol. 55 Globalisation
Vol. 56 The Wealth Divide
Vol. 57 Waste Pollution
Vol. 58 The Transport Issue
Vol. 59 Issues in Sport
Vol. 60 Confronting Cancer
Vol. 61 Fitness
Vol. 62 Drugs and the Law
Vol. 63 The Racism Debate
Vol. 64 The Gender Issue
Vol. 65 Human Rights
Vol. 66 Self-Esteem
Vol. 67 Parenting
Vol. 68 Coping with Depression
Vol. 69 The Media
Vol. 70 Adolescent Health
Vol. 71 Abortion

Vol. 72 Obesity and Eating Disorders
Vol. 73 Dealing with Bullies
Vol. 74 Money Matters
Vol. 75 Lone-Parent Families
Vol. 76 The Water Crisis
Vol. 77 Self-inflicted Violence
Vol. 78 Threatened Species
Vol. 79 Dealing with Homelessness
Vol. 80 The Cannabis Debate
Vol. 81 Alternative Therapies
Vol. 82 Protecting our Privacy
Vol. 83 Dealing with Crime
Vol. 84 Mental Wellbeing
Vol. 85 The Housing Crisis
Vol. 86 Smoking and your Health
Vol. 87 Genetic Modification
Vol. 88 Food and Nutrition
Vol. 89 Refugees
Vol. 90 Human and Animal Cloning
Vol. 91 Disability Issues

and stepfamilies **67**.13
and trans people **23**.28, 40
and the Universal Declaration of Human Rights **65**.29
views of long-married people **67**.1
young people's attitudes to **40**.8, 16, 28
massage **32**.27, 37-8, 40; **81**.4
maternity benefits **67**.8
maternity leave **25**.24, 25-6; **64**.11, 17
maternity pay **56**.16, 18
maternity rights **25**.18, 29
mealtimes **88**.1
meat consumption **88**.6, 26, 31
media
    and anti-globalisation protestors **55**.7
    and asylum seekers **63**.35
    and attitudes to teenage sexuality **75**.3
    and body image **72**.31, 34, 39
    and children's rights **65**.1, 3, 4
    Communications Bill **69**.16-20
    coverage of mental health issues **84**.21, 22
    and dieting **72**.35
    and the law **69**.31, 34, 35, 38-9
    and older people **16**.9, 12
    and pressure on athletes **59**.33-4
    and the reporting of suicides **77**.16, 20, 37
        and students **77**.22
    social effects of **69**.1-15
    teenage magazines **69**.33
    UK media ownership **69**.22-5
    see also advertising; Ofcom; television
medical abortion ('the abortion pill') **71**.1-2, 7, 10, 13, 22, 23
medicinal use of cannabis **80**.5, 7, 12, 22, 34, 35-9
    as an anti-emetic **80**.37
    as an appetite stimulant **80**.37
    and cannabinoids **80**.38
    and cannabis reclassification **80**.34
    Government policy on **80**.26, 34
    history of **80**.36
    and home cultivation **80**.32
    and intoxication **80**.39
    legality of **80**.38-9
    and multiple sclerosis (MS) **80**.35
    as a painkiller **80**.22, 26, 37
    public attitudes to **80**.36
    safety of **80**.38
    and smoking **80**.38
    and terminal illnesses **80**.37
    types of cannabis plants used in **80**.38
    and 'whole plant extract' **80**.38
melanoma (skin cancer) **28**.11-12; **60**.5, 18, 19-21
men
    and abortion
        abortions instigated by **71**.36
        information for **71**.26-7
        rights of fathers **71**.25
    age of marriage **40**.1, 3, 5, 6, 13, 20
        remarriage **40**.7
    and alcohol
        excessive drinking **39**.18
        health benefits **39**.37

    health risks **39**.10, 27
        recommended daily limits **39**.8, 9, 25
        and the workplace **39**.21
    attitudes of married men **40**.11
    and body image **72**.31
    body measurements of British men **61**.16
    and body-fat levels **61**.14-15
    and cancer **60**.3, 4, 5
    and child abuse **22**.1, 3, 4, 6, 10
    as childminders **22**.22
    and condom use **75**.15, 16
    and debt problems **43**.30
    and depression **68**.1
        stressful life events **68**.9
    and domestic violence **44**.5-6, 8-9, 18, 21, 27, 34-5, 38-40
    and eating disorders **72**.16, 20, 21, 30
    effects of anabolic steroids on **59**.24
    expenditure on toiletries **43**.2
    and extra-marital affairs **40**.7
    and gambling **29**.8, 26
    healthy diet guidelines for **61**.30, 37
    and healthy eating **72**.38
    and Internet access **31**.1
    Italian **67**.4
    life expectancy **16**.6, 7, 32
    living alone **16**.2, 3
    living in a partnership **67**.4
    male earning power and marriage **67**.33
    male pregnancy **11**.31, 40
    marital status **16**.2, 3
    and mental illness **84**.1
    missing persons **79**.13
    mortality rates **56**.1
    and obesity **61**.8
    part-time work **25**.1, 25
    and physical activity **61**.2, 4-5, 11
    retirement age **16**.26
    and self-harm **77**.14
    and sexual abuse **22**.15
    and sexually transmitted infections **10**.5, 10
    sharing responsibility for household chores **25**.16
    single homeless **79**.19
    and suicide **77**.2; **84**.1
    and university education **64**.8-9
    and vasectomies **75**.16
    and vegetarianism **19**.1
    and work-related stress **32**.30
    in the workforce
        and equal pay **64**.17
        and occupational choice **64**.13
        and the pay gap **64**.24
        salaries of male managers **64**.15, 16, 22, 23
menopause **11**.5, 14
mental health
    and abortion **71**.34-6
    and adolescents **70**.1, 3, 4, 6-7
    and alcoholism **39**.28
    and cannabis **80**.7, 10, 12, 13, 14, 16, 19-20, 26
    costs of mental health care **84**.1, 38
    education in **84**.4, 30-2

emotional health and wellbeing **84**.24

the government and the draft mental health bill **84**.36

and older people **16**.30, 31, 33, 34, 36-9

and self-esteem **66**.10, 12

and self-harm **77**.6-7, 8, 10, 11, 13

statistics **84**.1, 20

and suicide **77**.3

in the workplace **32**.11-12; **84**.23

mental illness

attitudes to **84**.4-5, 21-2

breakdowns **84**.4-5

campaigns to promote greater sensitivity **84**.22

and cannabis **62**.8, 27, 35; **68**.7

causes of **84**.9

characteristics of **84**.2-3

and children and young people in prison **83**.23

and complementary therapies **81**.21

defining **84**.8, 22

duration of **84**.9

effects on family members **84**.9-10

and film censorship **27**.7

genetic predisposition to **84**.5

and girls in prison **83**.27, 29

help for people with **84**.10

helping a friend **84**.20

and homelessness **79**.2, 10, 15, 16-17, 19, 32

and learning disabilities **84**.2

likelihood of suffering from **84**.4

and low incomes **56**.2

and missing persons **79**.13, 14

myths about **84**.23, 26

problems in the family **84**.8-10

recovery from **84**.5

as a stigmatising label **84**.22

and students **84**.32-3

and suicide **68**.10

symptoms of **84**.8-9, 20

and teenage girls **70**.31

treatment **84**.25, 27

types of **84**.1

and violence **84**.4, 18

and young people **84**.1, 5-6, 8-10, 13-15, 28, 30-2

see also depression; schizophrenia

migration

and housing areas in decline **85**.38

and population growth **20**.4-5, 6, 11

and population growth in the UK **85**.29, 30

replacement migration **20**.15-16

and worldwide poverty **56**.37

see also asylum seekers

milk **87**.27; **88**.6, 15

anti-milk campaign **19**.17, 18

cloning and milk proteins **90**.29-30, 32, 35

and lactose intolerance **19**.18

and vegan diets **19**.12, 16

minimum wage **25**.17; **43**.4; **56**.13, 18; **64**.22

and young people **75**.10

and young workers **25**.17

mobile phones

accessing the Internet through **31**.2, 3

bullying by **31**.21; **73**.3, 4

future of **31**.12

market for **43**.2, 10

and online gambling **29**.12, 13

policing **31**.35

recycling **57**.33

and the 'snoopers' charter' **82**.23

text messages, making payments using **31**.4

thefts of **83**.7, 18, 32

tracking of **82**.19-20

money

advice centres **43**.34

and the cashless society **74**.9-11

and children **74**.4, 5-6, 6-7, 12-13

financial planning **74**.14-39

and gender relationships **64**.36

and lone parents **75**.37-8, 39

public attitudes to **74**.5-6

students **74**.1, 17, 19-22, 28-32, 34-9

teenagers **74**.8-9

will making **74**.16

see also banks; incomes; wages

mortgages

and first-time buyers **85**.6, 7

Volume numbers appear first (in bold) followed by page numbers; a change in volume number is preceded by a semi-colon.

Vol. 3   The Animal Rights Debate

Vol. 4   The Euthanasia Issue

Vol. 10 Sexually Transmitted Diseases

Vol. 11 Fertility Rights

Vol. 16 Our Ageing World

Vol. 19 Looking at Vegetarianism

Vol. 20 Population Growth

Vol. 22 Confronting Child Abuse

Vol. 23 Sexuality

Vol. 25 The Changing Workplace

Vol. 27 The Censorship Issue

Vol. 28 The Global Warming Debate

Vol. 29 Gambling

Vol. 31 The Impact of the Internet

Vol. 32 Coping with Stress

Vol. 33 The Tourism Issue

Vol. 35 The Education Crisis?

Vol. 39 Alcohol Abuse

Vol. 40 The Future of Marriage

Vol. 43 A Consumer Society

Vol. 44 Confronting Domestic Violence

Vol. 46 Child Labour

Vol. 54 The Energy Debate

Vol. 55 Globalisation

Vol. 56 The Wealth Divide

Vol. 57 Waste Pollution

Vol. 58 The Transport Issue

Vol. 59 Issues in Sport

Vol. 60 Confronting Cancer

Vol. 61 Fitness

Vol. 62 Drugs and the Law

Vol. 63 The Racism Debate

Vol. 64 The Gender Issue

Vol. 65 Human Rights

Vol. 66 Self-Esteem

Vol. 67 Parenting

Vol. 68 Coping with Depression

Vol. 69 The Media

Vol. 70 Adolescent Health

Vol. 71 Abortion

Vol. 72 Obesity and Eating Disorders

Vol. 73 Dealing with Bullies

Vol. 74 Money Matters

Vol. 75 Lone-Parent Families

Vol. 76 The Water Crisis

Vol. 77 Self-inflicted Violence

Vol. 78 Threatened Species

Vol. 79 Dealing with Homelessness

Vol. 80 The Cannabis Debate

Vol. 81 Alternative Therapies

Vol. 82 Protecting our Privacy

Vol. 83 Dealing with Crime

Vol. 84 Mental Wellbeing

Vol. 85 The Housing Crisis

Vol. 86 Smoking and your Health

Vol. 87 Genetic Modification

Vol. 88 Food and Nutrition

Vol. 89 Refugees

Vol. 90 Human and Animal Cloning

Vol. 91 Disability Issues

and interest rates **85.**6

and single people **85.**7

mothers

  age of becoming a mother **67.**3, 4, 18, 36, 37

  and children's diets **72.**4

  domestic violence and mother/child relationship
    44.31, 32

  eating habits **72.**2

  full-time **67.**32-3

  and girls' perfectionism **70.**32

  lesbian **67.**16

  older **67.**36-7

  and suicidal young men **77.**33

  and the superwoman myth **67.**32

  support received from fathers **67.**11

  supporting and empowering **64.**2

  teenage mothers **70.**12

  time spent cooking **67.**2

mountain glacier melting **28.**10, 15, 17-18, 19-20, 26,
  30, 40

multiculturalism

  and British identity **63.**10, 26

  contradictions in multicultural Britain **63.**26

  defining **63.**4, 26

  on radio and TV **63.**9

N

natural gas **54.**3, 7

natural medicine *see* complementary medicine (CM)

nature trails, and responsible tourism **33.**27

naturopathy **81.**2, 19

neighbourhood strategies

  and housing **85.**14

  to combat racism **63.**31

neighbours, dealing with nuisance neighbours **83.**5, 6

nervousness, and self-confidence **66.**23

neuroblastoma in children **60.**9, 10

neurotic disorders

  depression **68.**18, 20

  prevalence of **68.**19

nicotine

  addiction **86.**2, 10

  effects of **86.**4

  gum **86.**26

  patches **86.**26

  replacement therapy **86.**3, 27, 37

  withdrawal symptoms **86.**30, 35, 36

nuclear energy **28.**9; **54.**1, 6-7, 7-9

  compared with wind power **54.**15, 16

  costs of **54.**5

  as a non renewable energy source **54.**2-3

  reprocessing nuclear fuel **54.**8, 9

  safety issues **54.**5, 8-9, 12

  statistics **54.**6

  in the UK **54.**6, 7, 8, 14, 22, 25, 40

  waste problems and management **54.**4, 5, 8, 9, 12, 25

  world producers of **54.**8

nudity

  in films **27.**20, 23, 24

on television **27.**28

numeracy skills, of adults in Britain **74.**32

nutritional therapy **81.**2

O

obesity **72.**1-14; **88.**4, 9-11

  and adolescent health **70.**4, 9, 27, 28, 29-30

  and attitudes to food **72.**33-4

  and Body Mass Index (BMI) **61.**14-15; **72.**6, 7, 12, 14

  in Britain and other European countries **61.**17

  in children **61.**1, 5-6, 7, 11, 12, 17, 35; **72.**4-5, 11;
    88.3, 11

    and bedroom TVs **61.**5

    and diabetes **61.**1, 6, 7, 11

    and diet **61.**17, 35

    and heart disease **61.**6

  controlling the global epidemic **72.**10

  defining **72.**7, 12

  and diet **61.**7, 8, 37

    in children **61.**6

    guidelines for the prevention of **61.**30-1

    market for diet food and drink **61.**17

  drugs **72.**5

  economic costs **72.**9, 12; **88.**4

  and fat distribution **61.**14; **72.**7

  and the food industry **72.**6, 11, 14

  in girls and young women **72.**1-3, 6

  and health **61.**6, 12, 37, 38; **72.**1, 8-9, 10, 12, 14, 37

  human cost of **72.**12

  increase in **61.**8

  and lifestyle **61.**8

  and overweight **72.**7-9

  and physical activity **61.**8-9, 26

  prevalence of **72.**5, 6, 8, 12, 14

  psychological aspects of **72.**9

  in Scotland **61.**11

  tackling obesity in England **72.**12

  and waist size **61.**15

  and young people **61.**2; **72.**6

  see also body weight

oceans

  coral reefs **28.**17

  desalination of sea water **76.**22

  endangered species **78.**3

  and global warming **28.**3-4, 14, 23

  marine life and tyre reefs **57.**8

  marine litter **57.**13

  pollution of **78.**6, 14

  sea level rises **28.**7, 9, 10-11, 15, 16, 17, 20, 23

  sea temperature measurements **28.**21

  wave power **54.**1, 3, 8, 10, 11, 13, 27

office workers

  attitudes to working from home **25.**27

  office/desk rage **32.**26, 30

oil

  environmental effects of oil production **55.**29-30

  and loans to developing countries **55.**34

  production of **54.**3, 4

  recycling **57.**23, 26, 33

spills **54.**5

world reserves of **54.**7-8

oil companies

and renewable energy sources **54.**24, 28, 38-40

and stress management **32.**27

optimism **66.**15-16

oral health **88.**17

oral sex, and HIV **10.**18, 21

organ transplants *see* therapeutic cloning

organic farming **87.**23-4, 28

organic food **88.**13-14, 18, 33, 34

organic waste **57.**1, 2

composting **57.**18, 19, 21, 22, 39

making your own compost **57.**24-5, 35

recycling **57.**5, 22

osteoarthritis, and obesity **72.**1, 9

osteopathy **81.**6-7, 23, 36

cranial **81.**2

defining **81.**3, 6

and the NHS **81.**4

regulation of **81.**7, 23

and scientists **81.**28, 29

osteoporosis **19.**17, 18; **61.**22, 26

and chiropractic **81.**9

ovarian cancer **11.**6; **60.**4, 11

overachievement, and low self-esteem **66.**3, 12

ovulation **11.**3, 7

and fertility treatment **11.**4, 8, 12

IUI **11.**11, 13, 28

oxygen deprivation **86.**4, 10

oxygen therapy **81.**3, 31, 33

ozone layer **28.**11-12, 25

P

package holidays

attitudes towards **33.**9-11

booking a holiday **33.**9-10

and 'customised' trips **33.**8

statistics **33.**4

packaging

EU legislation on **57.**14

and household waste **57.**15, 20, 22, 25

and litter **57.**10

plastics in **57.**31

recycling **57.**19, 22, 32

reducing the amount of **57.**20, 21, 25

reducing the weight of **57.**4

paedophiles **22.**28-40

characteristics of **22.**28

identification of in the US **22.**30, 32

on the Internet **22.**31-2, 33; **31.**22-3, 35-6

protecting children from **22.**28-9

and sex exploiters **46.**26

vigilante action against **22.**31

pain killers

cannabis as **80.**22, 26, 37

and euthanasia **4.**3, 4, 5-6, 7, 8, 15, 16, 20

palliative care

and euthanasia **4.**3, 4, 8, 9, 12, 16, 21

medical debate on **4.**23, 25, 26

paper

composting **57.**25

reducing the amount of waste paper **57.**21

paper recycling **57.**4, 23, 26

markets for **57.**18, 30

questions and answers **57.**34

statistics **57.**32

parenting **67.**17-39

advice for working mothers **67.**9-10

authoritative **67.**29

being a parent today **67.**17

classes **67.**22-3

confident parenting **67.**31

disciplining children **67.**20, 22

positive discipline **67.**31

and fathers **67.**11, 24-31

information on **67.**18

listening to parents **67.**18

midlife **67.**36-7

nine steps to more effective parenting **67.**20-1

permissive **67.**29

responsibility and young fathers **75.**12

Volume numbers appear first (in bold) followed by page numbers; a change in volume number is preceded by a semi-colon.

Vol. 3 The Animal Rights Debate	Vol. 44 Confronting Domestic Violence	Vol. 72 Obesity and Eating Disorders
Vol. 4 The Euthanasia Issue	Vol. 46 Child Labour	Vol. 73 Dealing with Bullies
Vol. 10 Sexually Transmitted Diseases	Vol. 54 The Energy Debate	Vol. 74 Money Matters
Vol. 11 Fertility Rights	Vol. 55 Globalisation	Vol. 75 Lone-Parent Families
Vol. 16 Our Ageing World	Vol. 56 The Wealth Divide	Vol. 76 The Water Crisis
Vol. 19 Looking at Vegetarianism	Vol. 57 Waste Pollution	Vol. 77 Self-inflicted Violence
Vol. 20 Population Growth	Vol. 58 The Transport Issue	Vol. 78 Threatened Species
Vol. 22 Confronting Child Abuse	Vol. 59 Issues in Sport	Vol. 79 Dealing with Homelessness
Vol. 23 Sexuality	Vol. 60 Confronting Cancer	Vol. 80 The Cannabis Debate
Vol. 25 The Changing Workplace	Vol. 61 Fitness	Vol. 81 Alternative Therapies
Vol. 27 The Censorship Issue	Vol. 62 Drugs and the Law	Vol. 82 Protecting our Privacy
Vol. 28 The Global Warming Debate	Vol. 63 The Racism Debate	Vol. 83 Dealing with Crime
Vol. 29 Gambling	Vol. 64 The Gender Issue	Vol. 84 Mental Wellbeing
Vol. 31 The Impact of the Internet	Vol. 65 Human Rights	Vol. 85 The Housing Crisis
Vol. 32 Coping with Stress	Vol. 66 Self-Esteem	Vol. 86 Smoking and your Health
Vol. 33 The Tourism Issue	Vol. 67 Parenting	Vol. 87 Genetic Modification
Vol. 35 The Education Crisis?	Vol. 68 Coping with Depression	Vol. 88 Food and Nutrition
Vol. 39 Alcohol Abuse	Vol. 69 The Media	Vol. 89 Refugees
Vol. 40 The Future of Marriage	Vol. 70 Adolescent Health	Vol. 90 Human and Animal Cloning
Vol. 43 A Consumer Society	Vol. 71 Abortion	Vol. 91 Disability Issues

parents
  and abortion **71**.36
  and advertisements targeting children **69**.12, 13
  and advertising aimed at children **43**.9
  and alcohol consumption **70**.20
  and arranged marriages **40**.21
  binding over **83**.25
  and child labour
    attitudes to education **46**.1
    domestic **46**.4-5
  and childhood depression **68**.6
  and childminders **22**.22, 23-4
  and children as consumers **43**.6, 7
  and children playing the National Lottery **29**.36
  and children's rights **65**.1, 4, 7
    donor-conceived children **65**.8-9
    parental responsibility (PR) **65**.11-12
  and children's self-esteem
    and discipline **66**.36
    improving **66**.36, 39
    and parenting style **66**.6, 8, 12-14, 29
    praising appropriate behaviour **66**.8-9, 36
  and computer games **27**.16, 17
  dealing with suspected child abuse **22**.21
  and divorce
    and the courts **40**.30-1
    helping children through **40**.35-6, 37-8
  and drugs
    advice for **62**.11
    attitudes to cannabis **62**.2
    campaigning for legalisation **62**.32
    support for **62**.16, 17
  and film censorship
    the '12' certificate **27**.4, 5
    and the Campaign against Censorship **27**.6, 7
  of gay people, and 'coming out' **23**.9, 10
  and the Internet **69**.3
    censorship **27**.10, 13
  and mobile phone tracking **82**.20
  and money matters
    savings **74**.7
    teaching children about **74**.1, 5-6
  needs and limitations of **67**.21
  and obesity in children **72**.5, 11
  older **67**.36-7
  and the physical punishment of children **22**.22, 23-4,
    25, 26, 27; **65**.7, 12, 13-14
  problem drinkers **39**.14, 30-2
  protecting children from paedophiles **22**.28-9, 35, 36
  and racism **63**.32
  and school bullying in Scotland **73**.16
  and self-harm by children **77**.25
  and smoking, children of parents who smoke **70**.19
  and spam (Unsolicited Bulk Emails) **82**.31
  staying together for the sake of the children **40**.39-40
  and stress in children **32**.8, 10
  and student money management **35**.33; **74**.19, 38
  and student support **35**.35, 37
  and suicidal feelings in young men **77**.33
  and suicide of children **77**.36-8
  taking children to school **58**.21
  teenage **70**.11-12
  and teenage drinking **39**.13, 20
  and teenage pregnancies **71**.9, 10, 12, 19
  and teenagers with depression **68**.30-1
  and television
    children's programmes **69**.6
    and family viewing time **69**.3
    soap operas **69**.8
  time spent with children **40**.1; **67**.2
  and truancy of children **35**.13, 15
  and university students **84**.33
  young offenders as **83**.23
  young people's respect for **83**.18
  see also birth parents; fathers; lone parents; mothers
part-time jobs **25**.1
  children and teenagers with **74**.6, 8, 9
  and children of working mothers **67**.34, 35, 38, 39
  and men **25**.1, 25
  and older people **16**.13
  and the pay gap **64**.19, 21, 25, 27
  and students **35**.26, 27, 29, 33, 34, 37, 40
  students with **74**.20, 37
  and women **25**.1, 6, 7, 25; **64**.10, 11, 12, 13, 34
passive smoking **86**.3, 12-13, 17-18, 23, 24-5
  and cancer **60**.16, 17
  and children **70**.19
passports **89**.33
  and identity cards **82**.9-10, 12
pedestrians
  and road accidents **58**.1, 20, 26
  safe and convenient routes for **58**.28
  street design for **58**.16
  and traffic speed **58**.14
pensions **16**.25-7; **89**.23
  basic state pension **16**.1, 27
  final salary pension schemes **16**.25
  increase in the number of pensioners **43**.3
  increase in pension age **16**.25, 26-7
  and life expectancy **16**.25, 26-7, 32
  pension scheme memberships **16**.9
  and statistical timebombs **16**.25
  and women **56**.15
  and workers in their 20s and 30s **16**.25
  and young managers **25**.23
  and young people **16**.27; **74**.1-2
pesticides **87**.7, 19, 23, 24, 25, 29; **88**.13, 32, 34, 35
pets
  and animal experiments **3**.7
  and animal rights **3**.4
  attacked by hounds **3**.28
  cloning **90**.30, 37, 38-9
physical abuse
  of children **22**.7, 9, 12, 13, 27; **44**.15-16
  and self-harm **77**.14
  and young runaways **79**.25
physician-assisted suicide (PAS) **4**.2, 10-12, 21
  and compassion **4**.10
  and the doctor-patient relationship **4**.29, 31
  effects on health professionals **4**.29
  and individual autonomy **4**.10-11
  legalisation of **4**.11

medical debate on **4.**24-6
oaths and declarations **4.**11
and patient rights **4.**28
Pill, contraceptive
and age of women **75.**15; **86.**9, 25
morning-after (emergency contraception) **75.**3, 13, 15-16, 17
and teenage pregnancies **75.**4
plants
for attracting butterflies **78.**35
endangered species **78.**2-3, 7
trade in **78.**17, 21
wildflowers **78.**36
lady's slipper orchid **78.**30
in tropical rainforests **78.**11
plastic recycling **57.**4, 13, 22
and energy production **57.**37
plastic bottles **57.**31
plastic cups **57.**33
products made from recycled plastic **57.**30, 31
reducing use of plastic **57.**13
plastics
biodegradable **57.**22
environmental taxes on bags **57.**15, 31, 32
production **87.**38
police
and alcohol-related violence **39.**19
and asylum communities **89.**20
and bullying **73.**14
and cannabis
guidelines on policing **80.**30, 31, 34
home cultivation of **80.**32-3
possession **80.**5, 7, 8, 23, 24-5, 30
powers of arrest **80.**30, 31, 34
reclassification **80.**29-30, 34
and under 18s **80.**7, 25, 30, 31, 34
and child abuse **22.**5, 17
and crime prevention **83.**32
and domestic violence **44.**3, 7-8, 10, 22-7
and driving by cannabis users **80.**21
drugs and the law **62.**18, 19
and football hooliganism **59.**11, 12, 13, 14-17, 18

and gun crime **83.**4
and homeless families **79.**36
and identity cards **82.**8
and the Internet
'anti-grooming' orders **22.**38, 39
and 'paedophile-free' chatrooms **22.**35
paedophiles **31.**35, 36
and the Internet Watch Foundation **31.**35
and racial harassment **63.**29
and racial violence **63.**13, 14
and racism
anti-racist course **63.**34-6
challenging racism in the police force **63.**33-6
and the criminal justice system **63.**17, 18
cultural quiz on **63.**35
in football **59.**8, 9, 10
and the McPherson Report **63.**13, 19, 29, 33, 34, 35
and the Race Relations Act (1976) **63.**35
racist attitudes **63.**34
stop and search practices **63.**17, 19, 33, 34
racism in the police force **83.**12
and reported crime **83.**2, 6, 7
shooting of police officers **83.**4
and suicide **77.**1, 36
and surveillance **82.**23
and traffic speed management plans **58.**31
and under-age drinking, test-purchasing methods of curbing **39.**12
and violent crime **83.**3, 4
and wildlife crime **78.**19, 39
working with to fight fraud **43.**36
and workplace bullying **73.**33
and yob-culture Britain **83.**6
and young runaways **65.**12; **79.**28-9, 31
and youth justice **83.**30
pollution
and children in the developing world **56.**22
and endangered species **78.**6
and energy efficiency **54.**30
and the Environment Agency **54.**3
and fossil fuels **54.**4, 28
and global warming **28.**3, 13, 23-4, 25-7, 39

Volume numbers appear first (in bold) followed by page numbers; a change in volume number is preceded by a semi-colon.

Vol. **3** The Animal Rights Debate
Vol. **4** The Euthanasia Issue
Vol. **10** Sexually Transmitted Diseases
Vol. **11** Fertility Rights
Vol. **16** Our Ageing World
Vol. **19** Looking at Vegetarianism
Vol. **20** Population Growth
Vol. **22** Confronting Child Abuse
Vol. **23** Sexuality
Vol. **25** The Changing Workplace
Vol. **27** The Censorship Issue
Vol. **28** The Global Warming Debate
Vol. **29** Gambling
Vol. **31** The Impact of the Internet
Vol. **32** Coping with Stress
Vol. **33** The Tourism Issue
Vol. **35** The Education Crisis?
Vol. **39** Alcohol Abuse
Vol. **40** The Future of Marriage
Vol. **43** A Consumer Society

Vol. **44** Confronting Domestic Violence
Vol. **46** Child Labour
Vol. **54** The Energy Debate
Vol. **55** Globalisation
Vol. **56** The Wealth Divide
Vol. **57** Waste Pollution
Vol. **58** The Transport Issue
Vol. **59** Issues in Sport
Vol. **60** Confronting Cancer
Vol. **61** Fitness
Vol. **62** Drugs and the Law
Vol. **63** The Racism Debate
Vol. **64** The Gender Issue
Vol. **65** Human Rights
Vol. **66** Self-Esteem
Vol. **67** Parenting
Vol. **68** Coping with Depression
Vol. **69** The Media
Vol. **70** Adolescent Health
Vol. **71** Abortion

Vol. **72** Obesity and Eating Disorders
Vol. **73** Dealing with Bullies
Vol. **74** Money Matters
Vol. **75** Lone-Parent Families
Vol. **76** The Water Crisis
Vol. **77** Self-inflicted Violence
Vol. **78** Threatened Species
Vol. **79** Dealing with Homelessness
Vol. **80** The Cannabis Debate
Vol. **81** Alternative Therapies
Vol. **82** Protecting our Privacy
Vol. **83** Dealing with Crime
Vol. **84** Mental Wellbeing
Vol. **85** The Housing Crisis
Vol. **86** Smoking and your Health
Vol. **87** Genetic Modification
Vol. **88** Food and Nutrition
Vol. **89** Refugees
Vol. **90** Human and Animal Cloning
Vol. **91** Disability Issues

individual actions to reduce **28**.27
and plastic bags **57**.32
and population growth **20**.14, 23, 24
and species extinction **78**.11
tourist-related **33**.29
population changes
decline in Europe **20**.4, 15
gender ratios **43**.2, 3
increase in the South East of the UK **43**.4
see also ageing population
population density
and hunger **56**.25
and refugees **89**.23
population growth **20**.1-40; **89**.31
and AIDS **20**.3, 5, 7, 11
and endangered species **78**.1
forecasting the next 25 years **20**.13-14
and global water shortages **76**.3, 5, 8, 15
and globalisation **55**.35
and immigration **20**.4-5, 11, 15-16, 32
and marriage rates **40**.5
and migration **85**.29, 30
and population density **20**.2
rates of **20**.1, 4, 7, 10, 20, 25, 26, 33, 36
stabilizing at sustainable levels **20**.20
and water consumption **76**.22, 29
pornography
and censorship **27**.31, 32
and children's rights **65**.2
on the Internet **27**.11-13, 38; **31**.23, 24, 27, 29, 31,
34-6
research into the effects of **27**.1
and sex on television **27**.27, 28
videos **27**.21
post-natal depression **68**.9, 11, 12, 14-16; **84**.7, 9, 19
causes of **68**.16
diagnosis of **68**.25
frequency of **68**.16
symptoms of **68**.15
treatment for **68**.15, 16
antidepressants **68**.15, 16, 36
poverty **56**.1-20; **91**.9
and adolescent health **70**.6, 7, 8
and affordable housing
in London **85**.10-12
in rural areas **85**.5
causes of **55**.37-8; **56**.5
and child labour **46**.1, 2, 3, 13; **65**.17
and child marriages **65**.18, 19
and child soldiers **46**.34
and child tax credit (CTC) **56**.16
and children's rights **65**.23
combating world poverty **55**.38
by increasing trade **55**.17
defining and measuring **55**.37; **56**.1, 2, 7, 8, 17
and depression in children and young people **68**.5
and drug abuse **62**.38
and elderly people **16**.7, 11, 17, 27; **56**.3, 14, 15
eradication **87**.28-30, 36
food and low-income families **61**.9
and globalisation **55**.1-2, 15, 20, 21-2, 27, 35-9

and homelessness **79**.4
and housing **79**.9
and international trade rules **55**.26
living below the poverty line **55**.37
and lone parents **75**.31, 32, 39
measuring **55**.37; **56**.1, 2, 7, 8, 17
and obesity **72**.1, 2
and population growth **20**.9, 33
reducing world poverty **33**.34
and the sexual exploitation of children **46**.26
and social exclusion **56**.1, 4, 7
and the Social Fund **56**.18, 19
and state benefits **56**.16, 18
and teenage pregnancy and parenthood **75**.1, 5, 10
and tourism **33**.32-3
ecotourism **33**.20, 25
pro-poor tourism **33**.34-5
and transport costs **58**.15
trends **55**.36
and water
and development aid **76**.30-1
and human rights **76**.25
multinational water corporations **76**.29
supplies in developing countries **76**.6
and women **56**.15
and the World Trade Organisation **55**.11, 33-4
and young motherhood **56**.13
pregnancy
abnormalities in, and surrogacy **11**.25
and alcohol consumption **39**.26, 28, 35-6
and anti-depressant drugs **68**.36
and cannabis **80**.15, 19
cannabis use in **62**.28
and domestic violence **44**.10, 18, 19, 25
ectopic **10**.6, 7, 11; **71**.16
health and safety in the workplace **64**.34
and HIV infection **10**.15, 16, 22, 30
increase in multiple births **67**.3
male **11**.31, 40
and miscarriage **71**.14
multiple **11**.24, 27
and sexually transmitted infections
abnormalities caused by **10**.13
chlamydia **10**.6
genital herpes **10**.8
gonorrhoea **10**.6, 7
tests for **10**.13
treatment **10**.13
and smoking **86**.4, 24, 25, 38; **88**.7
symptoms of **71**.12
testing **3**.22; **71**.9
unplanned **71**.12-13, 14, 16
unwanted **10**.1, 2, 11, 37
women in their forties **67**.36-7
primary schools
abuse of teachers in **73**.28
bullying in **73**.15
educational attainment **35**.6-7
ineffective **35**.16-17
and sex education **75**.24
teaching standards **35**.14

teaching of writing **35**.7, 17

prisoners

  background of and social exclusion **83**.8

  children in prison (under 18s) **83**.23

  costs of prison **83**.8

  families of **83**.39

  girls under 18 in prison custody **83**.23, 27-9

  and the Home Detention Curfew (HDC) **83**.9

  and life in prison **83**.10

  long-term **83**.9

  re-offending rates **83**.8, 10

  rise in the prison population **83**.9-10

  women **83**.9

  young people in prison (18-20 year olds) **83**.23

  youth justice and custodial sentences **83**.24, 25

prisons

  alternatives to custody **83**.34

  ethnic minorities and the criminal justice system **63**.18

  and Government drug strategy **62**.17

  imprisonment of children **65**.2, 5, 15

  self-esteem programmes in **66**.20

  sentences for cannabis possession **80**.30, 34

  suicides **70**.36

privacy

  aspects of **65**.36-7

  children's right to **65**.1, 4

  and human rights **65**.36-7

  and the Human Rights Act **65**.24-5

  and the media **69**.38-9

privacy rights **82**.1-3, 39

  and air travel **82**.3

  bodily privacy **82**.5

  and communications data **82**.1-2

  communications privacy **82**.5

  comprehensive laws on **82**.5

  defining privacy **82**.4

  and human rights **82**.4-5, 18

  information privacy **82**.5

  models of privacy protection **82**.5

  sectoral laws on **82**.5

  and self-regulation **82**.5

  and technologies of privacy **82**.5

territorial privacy **82**.5

viewpoints on privacy **82**.4

in the workplace **82**.25-30

see also identity (ID) cards; surveillance

private sector

  absenteeism **25**.14

  and long working hours **25**.6

prostate cancer **60**.3, 4, 6, 24-5

  causes and prevention **60**.24

  incidence of **60**.25

  symptoms **60**.24

  treatment **60**.24, 25, 35

prostitution

  and child marriages **65**.18

  and children's rights **65**.2

psychotherapy **32**.7, 17

  cognitive behaviour therapy (CBT) **84**.35

  and low self-esteem **66**.3, 7, 12

  and mental illness **84**.10

  and seasonal affective disorder **68**.21

  as a treatment for depression **68**.10, 13, 31

puberty and self-esteem **66**.31

public attitudes

  to abortion **71**.2-3, 16, 30

  to advertising **69**.14-15

  to AIDS/HIV **10**.14-15, 20

  to alcohol **39**.2-3, 19, 22, 24

  to animal experiments **3**.22

  to censorship

    BBFC guidelines **27**.3, 22, 31

    broadcasting regulation **27**.18

    of films on television **27**.29

    and strong language **27**.38-9

  to childminders and disciplining children **22**.23-4

  to consumer rights **43**.14, 15-16

  to crime **43**.4

  to e-mail **31**.17

  to euthanasia **4**.22, 39

  to extra-marital affairs **40**.7

  to foxhunting **3**.31, 35, 36

  to globalisation **55**.7, 16

  to GM foods **87**.3-4, 5-7, 16

Volume numbers appear first (in bold) followed by page numbers; a change in volume number is preceded by a semi-colon.

Vol. 3   The Animal Rights Debate

Vol. 4   The Euthanasia Issue

Vol. 10 Sexually Transmitted Diseases

Vol. 11 Fertility Rights

Vol. 16 Our Ageing World

Vol. 19 Looking at Vegetarianism

Vol. 20 Population Growth

Vol. 22 Confronting Child Abuse

Vol. 23 Sexuality

Vol. 25 The Changing Workplace

Vol. 27 The Censorship Issue

Vol. 28 The Global Warming Debate

Vol. 29 Gambling

Vol. 31 The Impact of the Internet

Vol. 32 Coping with Stress

Vol. 33 The Tourism Issue

Vol. 35 The Education Crisis?

Vol. 39 Alcohol Abuse

Vol. 40 The Future of Marriage

Vol. 43 A Consumer Society

Vol. 44 Confronting Domestic Violence

Vol. 46 Child Labour

Vol. 54 The Energy Debate

Vol. 55 Globalisation

Vol. 56 The Wealth Divide

Vol. 57 Waste Pollution

Vol. 58 The Transport Issue

Vol. 59 Issues in Sport

Vol. 60 Confronting Cancer

Vol. 61 Fitness

Vol. 62 Drugs and the Law

Vol. 63 The Racism Debate

Vol. 64 The Gender Issue

Vol. 65 Human Rights

Vol. 66 Self-Esteem

Vol. 67 Parenting

Vol. 68 Coping with Depression

Vol. 69 The Media

Vol. 70 Adolescent Health

Vol. 71 Abortion

Vol. 72 Obesity and Eating Disorders

Vol. 73 Dealing with Bullies

Vol. 74 Money Matters

Vol. 75 Lone-Parent Families

Vol. 76 The Water Crisis

Vol. 77 Self-inflicted Violence

Vol. 78 Threatened Species

Vol. 79 Dealing with Homelessness

Vol. 80 The Cannabis Debate

Vol. 81 Alternative Therapies

Vol. 82 Protecting our Privacy

Vol. 83 Dealing with Crime

Vol. 84 Mental Wellbeing

Vol. 85 The Housing Crisis

Vol. 86 Smoking and your Health

Vol. 87 Genetic Modification

Vol. 88 Food and Nutrition

Vol. 89 Refugees

Vol. 90 Human and Animal Cloning

Vol. 91 Disability Issues

to health and ageing **16.**34
to homeless people **79.**4, 32
to lesbians and gay men **23.**16
to living wills **4.**40
to marriage **40.**3, 19
to money matters **74.**5-6
to online banking **31.**4
to online shopping **31.**4
to radio **69.**3
to refugees **89.**17
to responsible tourism **33.**10-11, 17, 18, 21, 37
to speed management and road safety **58.**30
to street issues **58.**25
to television **69.**1-3
to transport **58.**3, 7
to wind power **54.**15, 16, 17, 40
public sector housing *see* social housing
public sector workers
    absenteeism **25.**14
    affordable housing for **85.**1, 3, 20
    long working hours **25.**6
public smoking **86.**3, 13, 18, 19-23
public transport
    and air pollution **58.**8
    benefits of **58.**2
    and bicycles **58.**28
    and older people **16.**28
    and parents with young children **67.**8
    park and ride schemes **58.**3, 29
pubs **86.**17, 19, 20-3

Q

qualifications of refugees **89.**34-5
quitting smoking **86.**3, 6, 9, 14, 27-30, 33-7

R

racial harassment
    defining **63.**29
    and the Race Relations Act **63.**28, 29
    of refugees **89.**19, 20
    reporting incidents of **63.**29
racial violence **63.**4, 7, 13-15
    and the Race Relations Act **63.**28-9
racism
    and British identity **63.**38
    challenging **63.**1, 26-39
    and children **63.**1-2
    defining **63.**1, 4, 27
    and education **63.**11-12
    effects of **63.**1
        body image and self-esteem **66.**32
    in football **59.**1-11
    history of in the UK **63.**35, 36
    institutional **63.**4, 33
    on the Internet **27.**10; **31.**28-9
    and prejudice **63.**4
    public attitudes to in the UK **63.**5

and the Race Relations (Amendment) Act (2000)
        63.1, 19, 27-9
    racist language **27.**38
    reasons for **63.**1
    and stereotyping **63.**4
    white people as victims of **63.**15-16
    in the workplace **63.**5
racist bullying
    and the Commission for Racial Equality **73.**38
    of girls and young women **73.**6
    in schools **63.**2, 12; **73.**17
radio
    access to via television sets **69.**3
    advertising **69.**28, 29, 37
    interviews with criminals **69.**37
    and Ofcom **69.**27
    public attitudes to **69.**3
    taste and decency on **69.**36-7
    the UK radio market **69.**21, 22
railways
    compared with air travel **58.**18
    progress and problems with **58.**13-14
    public attitudes to **58.**3
    rail fares **58.**11, 14
rainfall
    and the renewal of freshwater **76.**9
    and water distribution in the UK **76.**1-2
rainforests
    destruction of **78.**11
    threatened species of animals in **78.**1, 5
rape
    and abortion **71.**3, 18, 21, 24
    and domestic violence **44.**10, 11, 18
recycling **57.**4, 14-18, 19, 22-36
    aluminium **57.**2, 4, 22-3, 27, 30
    at school **57.**21
    banks **57.**24
    books **57.**33
    cans **57.**22, 23, 27, 30
    car tyres **57.**8
    CDs **57.**33
    clothes **57.**35-6
    commercial waste **57.**30
    community schemes **57.**31
    computers **57.**33
    and the Ecoteam programme **57.**38
    electrical appliances **57.**33
    and the EU landfill directive **57.**6
    furniture **57.**33
    Government policies on **57.**14, 15, 16, 17, 20, 29, 30
    household waste **57.**4, 5, 16, 17, 20, 21, 22-3
    industrial waste **57.**23
    in Ireland **57.**14, 15, 31
    kerbside collections **57.**17, 18, 24, 27
    and the manufacturing process **57.**30
    markets for recycled material **57.**18, 20, 30
    metals **57.**22, 26
    mobile phones **57.**33
    motor vehicles **58.**35
    organic waste **57.**5, 22
    packaging **57.**19, 22, 32

plastic **57.**4, 13, 22, 30, 31, 33, 37
proportion of rubbish recycled **57.**29
public attitudes to **57.**16
role of **57.**26
spectacles **57.**33
technology **57.**26
tips **57.**20-1, 25
tools **57.**33
and zero waste policies **57.**39
redundancy **16.**13, 20
and age discrimination **16.**13, 20
and older workers **16.**17, 18
and structural adjustment policies **55.**2
and young workers **25.**17-18
reflexology **81.**3, 15-17, 23, 36
and the NHS **81.**17, 31
and stress-related illnesses **81.**16
training as a reflexologist **81.**16-17
refugees
children's rights **65.**1, 5, 15
and education **63.**11
older people **16.**7
and population growth **20.**11
and reproductive rights **20.**27
see also asylum seekers
refuges **44.**3, 5, 7, 8, 27, 28, 29-30, 32, 33, 36-8
accommodation in **44.**29-30, 33, 36
applying for rehousing **44.**37-8
children and young people in **44.**3, 5, 8, 29-30, 32, 36
and confidentiality **44.**36-7
for ethnic minority women **44.**28, 36
friendships in **44.**38
getting in to a refuge **44.**36
length of stay in **44.**36
numbers turned away from **44.**38
numbers of women and children in **44.**3, 7, 8
problems of living in **44.**8
returning home from **44.**37
rules in **44.**36
in Scotland **44.**36-8
relaxation
and anxiety **32.**7

and stress control **32.**17, 20, 25, 31, 33, 35, 36
techniques **66.**5
religion
and animal welfare **3.**1
and child marriages **65.**18
and children's rights **65.**1, 4, 7
combating racism in religious communities **63.**31
and the Communications Bill **69.**20
and ethnic minorities
and the law **63.**21
separate religious schools **63.**12
statistics **63.**3
and euthanasia **4.**2, 3, 5-6, 10
and homosexuality **23.**5, 8, 12, 18, 24-6
and job discrimination **23.**32-3
and the Human Rights Act **65.**25
and overpopulation **20.**3
and students **35.**34
and wedding ceremonies **40.**5, 13, 14, 15, 18, 20
religious views on abortion **71.**3, 8, 14-16, 17, 36
and the personhood of the fetus **71.**15, 17
and the soul **71.**14-15
renewable energy sources **28.**9, 27, 30; **54.**1, 3, 29, 38-40
bioenergy **54.**11, 12, 19
consumption of **54.**4
costs and subsidies **54.**22, 23, 36
and energy efficiency **54.**28-9
government policies on **54.**10, 14, 17, 22, 36
green electricity **54.**22, 31, 36-7
as a percentage of energy consumption **54.**3-4, 16
in the UK **54.**7, 8, 10-13, 25
reproductive rights **20.**27-8, 35-8
responsibilities
and child participation **65.**21
and children's rights **65.**6
and the Human Rights Act **65.**25-6
responsible tourism **33.**13-40
and air travel **33.**17
and biodiversity **33.**23, 24
challenge of **33.**14
defining **33.**13
and developing countries **33.**18, 32-3

Volume numbers appear first (in bold) followed by page numbers; a change in volume number is preceded by a semi-colon.

Vol. 3   The Animal Rights Debate
Vol. 4   The Euthanasia Issue
Vol. 10   Sexually Transmitted Diseases
Vol. 11   Fertility Rights
Vol. 16   Our Ageing World
Vol. 19   Looking at Vegetarianism
Vol. 20   Population Growth
Vol. 22   Confronting Child Abuse
Vol. 23   Sexuality
Vol. 25   The Changing Workplace
Vol. 27   The Censorship Issue
Vol. 28   The Global Warming Debate
Vol. 29   Gambling
Vol. 31   The Impact of the Internet
Vol. 32   Coping with Stress
Vol. 33   The Tourism Issue
Vol. 35   The Education Crisis?
Vol. 39   Alcohol Abuse
Vol. 40   The Future of Marriage
Vol. 43   A Consumer Society

Vol. 44   Confronting Domestic Violence
Vol. 46   Child Labour
Vol. 54   The Energy Debate
Vol. 55   Globalisation
Vol. 56   The Wealth Divide
Vol. 57   Waste Pollution
Vol. 58   The Transport Issue
Vol. 59   Issues in Sport
Vol. 60   Confronting Cancer
Vol. 61   Fitness
Vol. 62   Drugs and the Law
Vol. 63   The Racism Debate
Vol. 64   The Gender Issue
Vol. 65   Human Rights
Vol. 66   Self-Esteem
Vol. 67   Parenting
Vol. 68   Coping with Depression
Vol. 69   The Media
Vol. 70   Adolescent Health
Vol. 71   Abortion

Vol. 72   Obesity and Eating Disorders
Vol. 73   Dealing with Bullies
Vol. 74   Money Matters
Vol. 75   Lone-Parent Families
Vol. 76   The Water Crisis
Vol. 77   Self-inflicted Violence
Vol. 78   Threatened Species
Vol. 79   Dealing with Homelessness
Vol. 80   The Cannabis Debate
Vol. 81   Alternative Therapies
Vol. 82   Protecting our Privacy
Vol. 83   Dealing with Crime
Vol. 84   Mental Wellbeing
Vol. 85   The Housing Crisis
Vol. 86   Smoking and your Health
Vol. 87   Genetic Modification
Vol. 88   Food and Nutrition
Vol. 89   Refugees
Vol. 90   Human and Animal Cloning
Vol. 91   Disability Issues

and endangered species **33.**27, 28
and environmental regulations **33.**25
and human rights **33.**24, 25
local communities and cultural heritage **33.**24, 25
pro-poor **33.**34-5
and tour operators **33.**25, 32, 33, 37
travel guidelines **33.**26-7
and wildlife **33.**4, 27, 28, 29
restorative justice **83.**37-8
and school bullying **73.**19
retirement
attitudes to early retirement **16.**15
flexible **16.**19
increase in age of **16.**25, 26-7
official retirement age **16.**16, 27
see also pensions
companies making or using **82.**13, 15-16, 35
and crime **82.**17
and data protection **82.**16
defining **82.**13, 15
disabling **82.**14
in Euro banknotes **82.**14, 16
and function creep **82.**17
identifying **82.**13-14
media coverage of **82.**15
possible consumer benefits of **82.**16-17
safety of **82.**17
in shoes **82.**14-15
and surveillance **82.**16
road accidents
and cannabis **80.**16, 17
and children **58.**1, 15, 20
in deprived areas **58.**15
and the removal of traffic controls **58.**26
and road maintenance **58.**12
and speed **58.**30
road safety **58.**1
and children **58.**19, 21-3
health and fitness **58.**5
public attitudes to **58.**3
and speed management plans **58.**30-1
robberies
and gun crime **83.**4
mobile phone thefts **83.**7, 18, 32
rates of **83.**3
rough sleepers
backgrounds of **79.**10, 18
health problems of **79.**15
and homelessness **79.**20
missing persons **79.**14
numbers of **79.**1, 2, 5, 7, 8, 19
and the 'revolving door' syndrome **79.**32
in Scotland **79.**10
young people **79.**22, 23
see also homelessness
rural areas
and alcohol consumption **39.**10
crime in **83.**2
and global water supplies **76.**6, 7, 19-20
household expenditure in **43.**13; **56.**12
Internet access in **31.**10-11

and the Living Streets Campaign **58.**24-5
speed limits in **58.**28
transport in **58.**9
rural communities **88.**34
rural housing
affordable housing in **85.**5, 28, 31
and brownfield building **85.**28, 34
and the exception site policy **85.**28
and poverty **85.**5
and redundant farm buildings **85.**28
and wildlife **85.**33

S

salmonella **88.**28
salt intake **88.**2, 7, 10, 16, 23, 26
sanitation
in developing countries **76.**7, 8, 12, 17, 21
and the right to water **76.**24
savings
attitudes to **74.**5
and parents **74.**7
savings accounts
and teenagers **74.**8-9
and young people **74.**15
schizophrenia **84.**8, 13-15
and alcohol **84.**14
and cannabis **62.**8; **68.**7; **80.**7, 10, 12, 14, 17, 19-20, 22, 26
and childhood disorders **84.**29
and children in prison **83.**23
and depression **68.**19
and diet **84.**14-15
and drug abuse **84.**14
in everyday language **84.**2
genetic component in **84.**14
and smoking **84.**14
stigma attached to **84.**20
and suicide **68.**10; **77.**3, 18
symptoms **84.**2-3, 4, 9
and university students **84.**32
and violence **84.**18
school bullying **35.**13; **73.**1-24
abuse of teachers by pupils **73.**28
admitting to bullying and help with stopping **73.**9-10
anti-bullying policies **73.**7, 15, 17, 20, 24
boys **73.**5, 6, 11
bystanders **73.**24
characteristics of bullies **73.**22
and children with learning disabilities **73.**12-13
defining **73.**5, 13, 22
girls and young women **35.**13; **73.**5-7
helping victims of **73.**14
homophobic **23.**18, 31; **73.**6, 11
and mobile phones **73.**3, 4
online **73.**3
peer support **73.**15, 16, 24
and physical punishment **65.**14
reasons for **73.**13, 22
resisting the temptation to be a bully **73.**23

responses to
    anti-bullying policies **73**.7, 15, 17, 20, 24
    assertiveness techniques **73**.21
    bully boxes **73**.20, 24
    classroom 'courts' **73**.19, 20
    counselling **73**.24
    gang bullying **73**.21
    Government policies on **73**.7, 8
    guide to beating **73**.20-1
    helping schools to tackle bullying **73**.23-4
    peer support **73**.15, 16, 24
    pupil councils **73**.24
    raising awareness **73**.24
    schools' approach to **73**.7
    standing up for yourself or a friend **73**.22-3
    telling a teacher **73**.14, 15, 23
    what to do/what not to do **73**.8
schools' failure to deal with **73**.15
in Scotland **73**.16, 24
and Section 28 **73**.11
and self-harm **77**.6, 7, 9
streetwise guide to coping with **73**.13-14
talking to an adult about **73**.18
and truanting **73**.7
websites on **73**.18
and workplace bullying **73**.31
and young people's rights **73**.17-18
school exclusions **35**.4, 15; **56**.2, 3
    and alcohol **39**.14
    and cannabis **80**.7
    and gender **64**.8
    and prisoners **83**.8
    and race **35**.13; **63**.11
    and teenage parenthood **70**.12
    and young offenders **83**.14, 15
schools
    and children in developing countries **76**.13-14
    children walking to school **72**.2
    and children's rights **65**.2
    and children's self-esteem **66**.2
    combating racism in **63**.31, 32, 39
    computers in **31**.5, 8; **35**.25

drug abuse in **83**.12
drug use
    in England **62**.4-5
    and zero tolerance policies **62**.9
and education on AIDS/HIV **10**.25
and emergency contraception **75**.17
and ethnic minority children
    educational performance **63**.11, 12
    and English as an additional language **63**.12
    in mainly white schools **63**.12
    racist bullying in **63**.2, 12, 32
    separate schools for **63**.11-12
examination performance **35**.7-11, 12, 17
family planning provision in **71**.28
and the gender pay gap **64**.28
government funding for school buildings **35**.25
independent **35**.4, 7
and the Internet **27**.11-12; **31**.5, 8, 23-4
journeys to **58**.19-23, 28
and learning in the family environment **43**.7-8
and mental health
    education in **84**.30, 31
    positive steps to **84**.27
overcoming sex stereotyping in **64**.37
participation in school sports **72**.2-3
performance tables **35**.5
and physical education **61**.1, 3, 10
physical education in **70**.5
reducing, reusing and recycling waste in **57**.21
and safety on the Internet **31**.23-4
self-harm in **77**.30-1
sex education *see* sex education
specialist **35**.5
standards in state schools **35**.20
stress in school pupils **32**.9-10
and suicidal young men **77**.33
teaching about money matters **74**.1, 6, 12, 32-3
and teenage pregnancy as a 'career' choice **75**.14
transport to school **70**.26
truancy and offending **83**.14
water conservation in **76**.39
scratchcards

Volume numbers appear first (in bold) followed by page numbers; a change in volume number is preceded by a semi-colon.

Vol. 3 The Animal Rights Debate	Vol. 44 Confronting Domestic Violence	Vol. 72 Obesity and Eating Disorders
Vol. 4 The Euthanasia Issue	Vol. 46 Child Labour	Vol. 73 Dealing with Bullies
Vol. 10 Sexually Transmitted Diseases	Vol. 54 The Energy Debate	Vol. 74 Money Matters
Vol. 11 Fertility Rights	Vol. 55 Globalisation	Vol. 75 Lone-Parent Families
Vol. 16 Our Ageing World	Vol. 56 The Wealth Divide	Vol. 76 The Water Crisis
Vol. 19 Looking at Vegetarianism	Vol. 57 Waste Pollution	Vol. 77 Self-inflicted Violence
Vol. 20 Population Growth	Vol. 58 The Transport Issue	Vol. 78 Threatened Species
Vol. 22 Confronting Child Abuse	Vol. 59 Issues in Sport	Vol. 79 Dealing with Homelessness
Vol. 23 Sexuality	Vol. 60 Confronting Cancer	Vol. 80 The Cannabis Debate
Vol. 25 The Changing Workplace	Vol. 61 Fitness	Vol. 81 Alternative Therapies
Vol. 27 The Censorship Issue	Vol. 62 Drugs and the Law	Vol. 82 Protecting our Privacy
Vol. 28 The Global Warming Debate	Vol. 63 The Racism Debate	Vol. 83 Dealing with Crime
Vol. 29 Gambling	Vol. 64 The Gender Issue	Vol. 84 Mental Wellbeing
Vol. 31 The Impact of the Internet	Vol. 65 Human Rights	Vol. 85 The Housing Crisis
Vol. 32 Coping with Stress	Vol. 66 Self-Esteem	Vol. 86 Smoking and your Health
Vol. 33 The Tourism Issue	Vol. 67 Parenting	Vol. 87 Genetic Modification
Vol. 35 The Education Crisis?	Vol. 68 Coping with Depression	Vol. 88 Food and Nutrition
Vol. 39 Alcohol Abuse	Vol. 69 The Media	Vol. 89 Refugees
Vol. 40 The Future of Marriage	Vol. 70 Adolescent Health	Vol. 90 Human and Animal Cloning
Vol. 43 A Consumer Society	Vol. 71 Abortion	Vol. 91 Disability Issues

age restrictions **29.**27
expenditure on **29.**9
odds of winning **29.**2
percentage of the population buying **29.**7, 8
and problem gamblers **29.**9, 26
seasonal affective disorder (SAD) **68.**9, 11, 12, 20-1; **84.**7, 17, 19
self-employment **25.**1, 9
and gender **64.**13
and older people **16.**13, 23
self-esteem
and adolescent health **70.**6
answering misconceptions about **66.**7-9
and approval from 'significant others' **66.**8
and body image **72.**31-2
building up **66.**2, 12-14
and children **66.**1-2, 8-9, 12-14, 27-30, 36-8
and college students **66.**18
developing skills and **66.**5, 12, 28
downgrading **66.**11
and eating disorders **66.**10-11; **72.**29
and emotional health and wellbeing **84.**24
importance of **66.**1
improving **66.**27-8
nurturing children's **67.**20
the perfect self-esteem trap **66.**5
and post-abortion trauma **71.**33
psychological perspectives on **66.**20-1
true meaning of **66.**20-1
and young people **66.**25-39
self-harm **70.**7, 36, 37-9; **77.**6-14, 24-31
age of self-harmers **77.**6
copycat incidents of **77.**14, 24
defining **77.**12
and depression **68.**10
educational programmes **70.**39
and EED (extreme eating disorder) **72.**25
and girls in prison **83.**27, 28-9
helping someone who self-injures **77.**13
and men **77.**14
methods of **70.**37; **77.**8, 24
myths about **77.**10, 11, 12-13, 26
prevention
changing A & E staff attitudes **77.**26
getting help **77.**8, 13, 28
help by friends and family **77.**28-9
help by parents and teachers **77.**25
helping yourself **77.**10, 27-8
and the Samaritans **77.**29
specialist help for **77.**25
thinking about stopping **77.**27
and young people **77.**24-5, 27-9
psychological profile of self-harmers **77.**14
reasons for **70.**37-8; **77.**6-7, 9, 12, 24, 27, 30
in schools **77.**30-1
self-help strategies for **77.**14
sources of help **70.**38, 39
statistics **77.**9, 10; **84.**1
and students **77.**22
and suicide **70.**38; **77.**8, 9, 11, 12, 21
typical background/history **77.**10

and victims of bullying **73.**6-7
and women **77.**12-14
self-help
books **66.**4, 17
and children with learning disabilities **73.**12-13
for controlling stress **32.**17
for depression **84.**35
groups for anxiety sufferers **32.**7
and manic depression **68.**34
and post-natal depression **68.**15
and smoking **86.**37
in the treatment of depression **68.**2, 13, 37
and young people **68.**28-9
services
consumer rights when buying a service **43.**18
rights of disabled people **91.**7, 8, 13-14
service sector job creation **25.**1
sex censorship
the '12' rating **27.**4, 20
arguments against **27.**38
campaign against **27.**6
public attitudes to **27.**3, 22
sexual violence **27.**21
and television **27.**27-9
and women **27.**32
sex discrimination
in the Army **73.**34
in the workplace **23.**34, 35
sex education **75.**2, 20, 21-2
and attitudes and beliefs **75.**18, 19, 21
Government policies on **23.**11
and homosexuality **23.**10-12, 13-14, 18
in primary schools **75.**24
and relationships education **75.**21, 22, 24
right of parents to withdraw children from **75.**24
and teenage pregnancy **70.**10; **75.**2-3, 13, 14, 20-2, 23
sex offenders
and abuse of trust **23.**39
and the child protection system **22.**30-1
convicted overseas **46.**24
dismissal from employment **23.**34
Government policies on **22.**39
and gross indecency **23.**39
treatment of **22.**5-6
see also paedophiles
sex workers, and AIDS/HIV **10.**32
sexual abuse **10.**1; **22.**1, 4, 14, 16, 18-19; **46.**19-27
and adolescent health **70.**7
behaviour following **46.**26
characteristics of abusers **22.**16, 18; **46.**26
child domestic workers **46.**5
child prostitution **46.**3, 9-10, 19, 27
and AIDS/HIV **46.**20, 21, 22, 26
protection of children from **46.**20
child protection registers **22.**11, 12
child soldiers **46.**21, 33, 40
child trafficking **46.**19, 19-23, 20, 21-2, 23, 27
and children's rights **65.**2, 5
effects on behaviour **22.**19
in the family **22.**13
and girls in developing countries **65.**19, 20

and girls in prison **83**.28
and globalisation **55**.1
and low self-esteem **66**.6, 12
numbers of children involved **46**.25
and poverty **46**.26
psychological damage caused by **46**.26
reasons for exploiting children **46**.22
and self-harm **77**.10, 14
and sex tourism **46**.20, 21, 24, 26
and siblings **22**.10, 15-16
signs and symptoms of **22**.6, 7
statistics **22**.2, 3, 10
and suicide in adolescents **70**.36
young abusers' projects **22**.15-16
young people **22**.13-14
and young runaways **79**.25
sexual behaviour
and abstinence education **75**.18, 26-7
in adolescence **70**.6, 10-11, 13
and alcohol **39**.14; **70**.7
attitudes to **27**.27; **75**.3
average age of starting sex **10**.2
as a cause of HIV **10**.21
and early sexual relationships **75**.17-19
masochism and self-harm **77**.11
and multiple sexual partners **75**.16
reducing chances of HIV infection **10**.9, 18-19
and sexual feelings **23**.2-3
and sexually transmitted infections **75**.16, 17-18
underage sex **75**.14, 17-18, 27
sexual bullying/harassment
of girls and young women **73**.5
in schools **73**.17
in the workplace **73**.36
sexual health **20**.27, 28, 33-5, 39-40
and adolescents **70**.3
clinics **10**.1, 4, 7, 9-10, 12, 13
consequences of poor **10**.1
education programmes **10**.25, 33, 38
inequalities in sexual ill health **10**.2
problems **10**.1
sexual intercourse

and the conception of children **11**.31, 33
and female infertility **11**.3, 5-6
sexuality
and gay parents **67**.16
and stepfamilies **67**.12
sexually transmitted infections (STIs) **10**.4-8
and abstinence education **75**.26
and adolescent health **70**.4, 9
avoiding **10**.4
and blocked fallopian tubes **11**.5
chlamydia **10**.1, 2, 5, 6, 11
common symptoms of **10**.4
genital herpes **10**.8, 12
genital warts **10**.7, 12
gonorrhoea **10**.1, 2, 3, 5, 6-7, 11
international comparisons **10**.1
knowledge of **75**.15-16
notifying partners **10**.13
rates of **10**.3, 5
and safer sex **10**.12-13
and sex education **75**.22
and sexual health clinics **10**.4
syphilis **10**.1, 5, 11
and teenage sex **75**.17-18
testing for **10**.12
treatment **10**.12
and women **10**.5, 6-7, 8, 9-10
worldwide prevention programmes **10**.36
worldwide statistics on **10**.37
and young girls **71**.11
and young people **10**.5
shopping
and budgeting **74**.23
and children **43**.6-8
for clothes **43**.5, 8, 11
complaints **43**.19, 22
and energy efficiency **54**.29-30
expenditure on luxuries **43**.1, 3
and family-friendly policies in Britain **67**.8
from home **82**.36-7
and money management **74**.17
online **31**.2, 4; **43**.23-4, 38-9, 40

Volume numbers appear first (in bold) followed by page numbers; a change in volume number is preceded by a semi-colon.

Vol. 3   The Animal Rights Debate
Vol. 4   The Euthanasia Issue
Vol. 10 Sexually Transmitted Diseases
Vol. 11 Fertility Rights
Vol. 16 Our Ageing World
Vol. 19 Looking at Vegetarianism
Vol. 20 Population Growth
Vol. 22 Confronting Child Abuse
Vol. 23 Sexuality
Vol. 25 The Changing Workplace
Vol. 27 The Censorship Issue
Vol. 28 The Global Warming Debate
Vol. 29 Gambling
Vol. 31 The Impact of the Internet
Vol. 32 Coping with Stress
Vol. 33 The Tourism Issue
Vol. 35 The Education Crisis?
Vol. 39 Alcohol Abuse
Vol. 40 The Future of Marriage
Vol. 43 A Consumer Society

Vol. 44 Confronting Domestic Violence
Vol. 46 Child Labour
Vol. 54 The Energy Debate
Vol. 55 Globalisation
Vol. 56 The Wealth Divide
Vol. 57 Waste Pollution
Vol. 58 The Transport Issue
Vol. 59 Issues in Sport
Vol. 60 Confronting Cancer
Vol. 61 Fitness
Vol. 62 Drugs and the Law
Vol. 63 The Racism Debate
Vol. 64 The Gender Issue
Vol. 65 Human Rights
Vol. 66 Self-Esteem
Vol. 67 Parenting
Vol. 68 Coping with Depression
Vol. 69 The Media
Vol. 70 Adolescent Health
Vol. 71 Abortion

Vol. 72 Obesity and Eating Disorders
Vol. 73 Dealing with Bullies
Vol. 74 Money Matters
Vol. 75 Lone-Parent Families
Vol. 76 The Water Crisis
Vol. 77 Self-inflicted Violence
Vol. 78 Threatened Species
Vol. 79 Dealing with Homelessness
Vol. 80 The Cannabis Debate
Vol. 81 Alternative Therapies
Vol. 82 Protecting our Privacy
Vol. 83 Dealing with Crime
Vol. 84 Mental Wellbeing
Vol. 85 The Housing Crisis
Vol. 86 Smoking and your Health
Vol. 87 Genetic Modification
Vol. 88 Food and Nutrition
Vol. 89 Refugees
Vol. 90 Human and Animal Cloning
Vol. 91 Disability Issues

and responsible tourism **33**.27
and water conservation **76**.27
single homelessness **79**.5-7
case studies **79**.6-7, 16-17
and concealed households **79**.5, 7, 19
costs of **79**.5-6
legal entitlements **79**.8
and mental health problems **79**.15, 16-17
as a significant problem **79**.4
statistics **79**.5, 7, 19
single people
growth in numbers **43**.2
and the housing market **85**.7, 23-4
living alone **85**.2
numbers of **67**.2
numbers of single-person households **75**.29
slavery **65**.34-5
bonded child labour **46**.8-9, 10
in cocoa plantations **46**.12, 14
domestic slaves in Britain **46**.15
products using slave labour **46**.11
smoking
and adolescent health **70**.4, 6, 7-8, 17-19
adult smokers **86**.1, 2, 6, 14
advertising cigarettes **86**.5, 8, 26
age groups of smokers **86**.1
and animal experiments **3**.13
anti-smoking campaigns **86**.6, 8
bans **86**.3, 13, 19-23, 38
benefits of smoking **86**.11
and cancer **60**.1, 2, 3, 14, 15-17, 27
and childminders **22**.22, 23
and children **86**.1, 8, 14-15, 24-5, 26
costs of **86**.7, 25, 33
cutting back **86**.16
deaths from **86**.2, 9, 10, 14, 16, 17
decline in **86**.1, 2-3
and diet **61**.13
and ethnic minorities **63**.7
first cigarette of the day **86**.2
and fitness **61**.39
and footballers **59**.39
government targets **86**.3, 39
health risks **86**.2, 3, 5, 6, 9-11, 13, 14-16, 24-5, 31
and image **86**.5
and life expectancy **16**.30; **86**.31
and obesity **72**.2
passive *see* passive smoking
price of cigarettes **86**.7, 25, 33
in public places **86**.3, 13, 18, 19-23
and schizophrenia **84**.14
and self-harm **77**.6, 13, 26
socio-economic groups **86**.1-2
statistics **86**.1-3, 14
stopping **86**.3, 6, 9, 14, 27-30, 33-7
and stress **32**.30, 33, 35, 36
and suicidal feelings in young men **77**.33
and teenagers **86**.1, 2, 5-7
withdrawal symptoms **86**.30, 35, 36
women smokers **86**.1, 2, 5, 9, 14, 24, 25, 38, 154
in the workplace **86**.17, 18, 19, 23, 25

social class
and attitudes to advertising **69**.14
and attitudes to physical activity **70**.24
and attitudes towards homosexuality **23**.17
and child abuse **22**.3, 13, 14
and educational achievement **64**.8, 9
and foxhunting **3**.31
and gambling **29**.3, 8, 13
and health **56**.2
and obesity **70**.30; **72**.1-2
and physical activity **61**.4-5
and sexual exploitation and abuse **46**.26
and teenage parenthood **75**.1
and teenage pregnancies **56**.2-3; **70**.11-12
young people and diet **70**.26
social exclusion **16**.3, 11
and children in prison **83**.23
and crime **83**.8
and crime prevention **83**.33
education and gender **64**.9
and obesity **72**.1
and older people **16**.3, 11
and poverty **56**.1, 4, 7, 9, 14, 19
and transport policies **58**.16
and young people in prison **83**.23
social housing **85**.3
and affordable housing **85**.8
and the environment **85**.15
and house-building in south-east England **85**.18
numbers of houses built **85**.3, 8
and the right-to-buy **85**.5, 11, 38
sport **61**.8
and ethnic minorities **63**.2
participation in **61**.2, 3
team sports **61**.21, 24
stem cell research **90**.3, 5, 13, 14, 15, 20-1, 22
blood stem cells **90**.22
for replacement tissue **90**.16
see also embryonic stem cells
stepfamilies **67**.1, 12-13, 27, 28
discipline in **40**.36
living with **40**.31-2, 34, 37
and parental responsibility **65**.11
relationships with **40**.36
rewards of **40**.36
and sexual abuse **40**.25
statistics **40**.2, 34
and suicidal feelings in young men **77**.33
and suicide of children **77**.38
stress **32**.1-40; **86**.11, 35
and alcohol consumption **32**.28, 33, 34, 35, 39
avoiding **32**.32-3
causes of **32**.35
and commuting **25**.10-11, 27 **32**.36-7
coping with **32**.31-40; **68**.2-3
defining **32**.1
and depression **68**.1, 2-3
effects of **32**.1, 16-17
emotional effects of **68**.3
and HIV-positive people **10**.28
and life events **32**.16, 21-2

and neurotic depression **68**.20
and personality type **32**.16, 22, 32
physical responses to **32**.1, 32, 34, 35-6
and self-injury **77**.27
stressful life events **68**.9
symptoms of **32**.17, 34
and women **32**.20, 30, 34-5
and working fathers **64**.35
and working mothers **67**.18, 32-3
and young people **32**.1-10
stress-related illness **32**.13, 16, 18, 19-20, 22, 28, 30
strokes
and diet **19**.18
and older people **16**.30-1
students **35**.26-40; **91**.35
accommodation **35**.26, 34
activities **35**.34
drop outs **35**.21, 27, 29
exclusions for non-payment of fees **35**.29
graduate recruitment **91**.19-20
hardship **35**.35
and mental illness **84**.32-3
money management for **35**.39-40
and money matters **74**.1, 17, 19-22, 28-32, 34-9
and part-time jobs **35**.26, 27, 29, 33, 34, 37
and post-graduate earnings **35**.32
in Scotland **74**.20, 37
and self-esteem **66**.18-19
and suicide prevention **77**.15-16, 22-3
wheelchair students **91**.36
women students **35**.7, 8-9, 35
substance abuse
and adolescent health **70**.4, 14
and homelessness **79**.2
and young runaways **79**.29
suicide **77**.1-2, 1-5, 15-23, 32-9
and abortion **71**.33, 35, 36
age and rates of **77**.2
and bullying in the Army **73**.34
and cannabis **80**.16
as a cause of death **77**.1, 2
and children **40**.25

counselling for families of suicides **77**.1
and depression **68**.10, 12, 26, 31
effect on family and friends **77**.35, 36
and gay people **23**.19
and girls in prison **83**.28
and homeless people **79**.32
and illness **77**.3
and individual autonomy **4**.7
inquests into **77**.1, 36-7
and the law **4**.8, 11
and low self-esteem **66**.6, 20
missing persons **79**.14
prevention
behavioural approaches **77**.3
environmental strategies **77**.3
helping a suicidal friend **77**.21
national suicide prevention strategy **77**.16, 19
and public policy **77**.17-18
self-help **77**.35
students **77**.15-16, 22-3
talking treatments **77**.35
treatment of mental disorders **77**.3
young men **77**.23
rise in UK rate of **56**.19
risk factors for **77**.2-3, 5
and the Samaritans **68**.3, 31
and self-harm **77**.8, 9, 11, 12, 21
social and environmental factors in **77**.3
statistics **77**.2, 4, 16; **84**.1
survivors of bereavement by **77**.39
taboos surrounding **77**.2
of teachers **32**.10
and university students **84**.32-3
warning signs of **77**.4
and young men **77**.1-2, 4, 17, 23, 32-3
and young people **32**.8, 9; **56**.3; **70**.1, 4, 6, 8, 36
supermarkets
buying patterns **43**.5
population per grocery superstore **43**.3
profits **43**.3
surrogacy **11**.18-25
and the child

Volume numbers appear first (in bold) followed by page numbers; a change in volume number is preceded by a semi-colon.

Vol. 3   The Animal Rights Debate
Vol. 4   The Euthanasia Issue
Vol. 10   Sexually Transmitted Diseases
Vol. 11   Fertility Rights
Vol. 16   Our Ageing World
Vol. 19   Looking at Vegetarianism
Vol. 20   Population Growth
Vol. 22   Confronting Child Abuse
Vol. 23   Sexuality
Vol. 25   The Changing Workplace
Vol. 27   The Censorship Issue
Vol. 28   The Global Warming Debate
Vol. 29   Gambling
Vol. 31   The Impact of the Internet
Vol. 32   Coping with Stress
Vol. 33   The Tourism Issue
Vol. 35   The Education Crisis?
Vol. 39   Alcohol Abuse
Vol. 40   The Future of Marriage
Vol. 43   A Consumer Society

Vol. 44   Confronting Domestic Violence
Vol. 46   Child Labour
Vol. 54   The Energy Debate
Vol. 55   Globalisation
Vol. 56   The Wealth Divide
Vol. 57   Waste Pollution
Vol. 58   The Transport Issue
Vol. 59   Issues in Sport
Vol. 60   Confronting Cancer
Vol. 61   Fitness
Vol. 62   Drugs and the Law
Vol. 63   The Racism Debate
Vol. 64   The Gender Issue
Vol. 65   Human Rights
Vol. 66   Self-Esteem
Vol. 67   Parenting
Vol. 68   Coping with Depression
Vol. 69   The Media
Vol. 70   Adolescent Health
Vol. 71   Abortion

Vol. 72   Obesity and Eating Disorders
Vol. 73   Dealing with Bullies
Vol. 74   Money Matters
Vol. 75   Lone-Parent Families
Vol. 76   The Water Crisis
Vol. 77   Self-inflicted Violence
Vol. 78   Threatened Species
Vol. 79   Dealing with Homelessness
Vol. 80   The Cannabis Debate
Vol. 81   Alternative Therapies
Vol. 82   Protecting our Privacy
Vol. 83   Dealing with Crime
Vol. 84   Mental Wellbeing
Vol. 85   The Housing Crisis
Vol. 86   Smoking and your Health
Vol. 87   Genetic Modification
Vol. 88   Food and Nutrition
Vol. 89   Refugees
Vol. 90   Human and Animal Cloning
Vol. 91   Disability Issues

implications for **11**.25
   legal status **11**.21, 23
commissioning couple **11**.18-19, 20, 21-2, 30
decisions made during the pregnancy **11**.24-5
ethics of **11**.19-20, 22, 27, 30, 32-3
and IVF **11**.18, 19, 20
law on **11**.18-19, 21-2, 23
and multiple pregnancies **11**.24
and risk **11**.22
surrogate mothers **11**.18, 20-1, 22
   contact with parents and child **11**.25
   criteria for becoming **11**.24
   full and partial surrogacy **11**.20
   health risks to **11**.24
   identity of **11**.22, 24, 25
   payment of **11**.18, 20, 22, 24
   problems for **11**.19, 20
   rights of **11**.18
surveillance **82**.17-19
   defining **82**.17
   directed **82**.17-18
   electronic surveillance and civil liberties **82**.19
   and facial recognition technology **82**.3
   and the Government **82**.1-3, 22, 23
   and the law **82**.18
   mass surveillance technologies **82**.1
   passive **82**.17
   and private sector companies **82**.3
sustainable development **20**.24; **54**.20
   and energy consumption **54**.6
   and global water supplies **76**.17, 31
   national strategies for **55**.21
   in the UK **54**.27, 54
   and water power **54**.13
sustainable housing **85**.1, 9
   in rural areas **85**.5
   and sustainable communities **85**.32, 38, 39
syphilis **10**.1, 5, 11

T

tar **86**.4, 10
   in herbal cigarettes **86**.37
   low tar cigarettes **86**.32
taxation
   and air transport **33**.17
   carbon taxes **28**.26
   child tax credit (CTC) **56**.16
   climate-change levy in the UK **28**.36, 37
   corporate taxes **55**.8, 11
   and ecotourism **33**.17, 21-2, 30, 31
   and emissions trading **28**.36-7
   environmental taxes **57**.15, 31, 32
   gambling **29**.2, 17, 23, 36
   and homosexual couples **40**.18
   and marriage **40**.13, 16, 20
   of tobacco **86**.7, 23, 25
   and unmarried couples **40**.18
teachers
   abuse of by pupils **73**.28

and AIDS/HIV **10**.38
assessment by **35**.5
and children of working mothers **67**.34
and classroom layout **35**.18, 19
and corporal punishment of children **65**.15
disabled teachers **91**.32
and duty of care **65**.11
helping victims of bullying **73**.14, 15, 23
non-contact time **35**.5
and self-harm by pupils **77**.25, 31
and sex education **23**.14, 18
shortage of **35**.14-15, 16-17
and suicidal young men **77**.33
supporting self-esteem **66**.7
technology
   and globalisation **55**.15, 35
   and work-related stress **32**.21, 28
teenage pregnancies **10**.2; **56**.2-3; **70**.4; **75**.1-14, 17-27
   and abortion **20**.30, 34; **67**.3, 4; **71**.5, 8-11, 28-9;
      75.1, 3-4, 17
   and abstinence education **75**.18, 26-7
   and access to family planning **71**.28-9
   adoption of children of **71**.10
   attitudes to **75**.3, 7-8, 10, 27
   and benefit cuts **75**.22
   birth rates **67**.3, 4, 6
   children of teenage mothers **75**.2, 7-8
   consequences for young parents and children **70**.12
   and domestic violence **44**.18
   and ethnic minorities **75**.2, 23
   factors associated with **75**.2, 5
   and family planning **20**.29-30, 34, 39
   and health **75**.1, 2
   international comparisons **75**.5
   and low self-esteem **66**.6, 20
   negative consequences of **75**.2
   and parenthood **70**.11-12
   and poverty **75**.1, 5, 10
   pregnancy testing **71**.9
   and relationships with fathers **67**.25
   and responsibility **71**.9
   rise in the 1980s **75**.4
   and single parents **75**.5
   and social class **56**.2-3
   social stigma attached to **75**.10
   and socio-economic background **75**.1-2
   statistics **71**.39; **75**.1, 4
   and teenage sex **75**.17
   trends in **75**.4
   and underage sex **75**.14, 17-18, 27
   young people 'at risk' **75**.9
   young people with learning disabilities **75**.24
   young people's attitudes to **75**.6
television **69**.1-15
   advertising **69**.12, 29
   cable, satellite and multimedia **69**.23-4
   and cannabis users **80**.9
   censorship **27**.2, 38-40
   consumer programmes **43**.19
   deregulation and digital television **43**.10-11
   digital **27**.28; **69**.1-2

and disabled people **91**.21-2, 23-4
documentaries **69**.7
drama **69**.7
and ethnic minorities **63**.9
films on **27**.6, 28-9
holiday programmes on **33**.10
interactive, and online gambling **29**.12, 13, 14-15, 19
news programmes **69**.1, 2, 17
obesity in children and bedroom TVs **61**.5
and older people **16**.9, 12
and political bias **69**.2
quality and standards on **69**.1, 2
reality television **86**.5
regulation **69**.2
terrestrial TV in the UK **69**.22-3
viewing habits and preferences **69**.2
terrorism
    and the Anti-Terrorism, Crime and Security Act
        (2001) **82**.18, 33, 34
    and aviation security **82**.3
    and human rights **65**.31-2
    and identity cards **82**.2, 9, 10, 11
    and Muslims **63**.22, 24, 25
    war on terror **89**.8
    and worldwide poverty **56**.35
testicular cancer **60**.5, 18, 26
    in children **60**.11, 12, 13
theft
    rates of **83**.1
    victims of **83**.7
therapeutic cloning **90**.3, 5, 6, 10, 14, 17, 19, 23, 33
    see also stem cell research
tobacco
    additives **86**.7
    and cannabis **62**.31
    consumption **86**.2
    young people and the law **62**.22
tobacco companies **86**.6-7, 8, 20-1
    and the hospitality trade **86**.17
    profits **86**.25
tourism **33**.1-40
    advice on buying exotic souvenirs abroad **78**.21

business of **33**.5
costs of holidays **33**.5
and the countryside **85**.33
cultural impacts of **33**.30
in developing countries **20**.18; **33**.38-40
economic impacts of **33**.30-1, 35
and employment **20**.18
environmental impacts of **33**.4, 29
    and sustainable development **33**.36
expenditure on **33**.6, 7, 15, 23, 34
    savings **33**.12
growth of global tourism **33**.1-2, 6
highlights **33**.6-7
industry organisations **33**.2
sex tourism **46**.20, 21, 26
    British sex tourists **46**.24
statistics **33**.4
where tourists come from **33**.1-2
workforce employed in **33**.1, 15, 23
    see also ecotourism; responsible tourism
toxic chemicals
    and car tyres **57**.7-8
    and incinerated waste **57**.6
    testing **3**.8, 21
    and water pollution **76**.11
trade in endangered species **78**.16-17, 19-22
    and traditional medicine **78**.23
    and the UK **78**.38-9
tranquillizers **32**.7, 20; **62**.4, 7, 21
trans people **23**.27-8
    and marriage **23**.40
transplant organs
    and animal experiments **3**.14
    and cloning **90**.20, 22
    xeno-transplantation **90**.30, 32-3
transport
    and climate change **28**.27, 30, 34; **58**.1, 5, 8-9
    and the costs of commuting **25**.10-11
    and energy efficiency **54**.29, 31
    Government policies on **58**.5, 7, 11, 13, 14
    integrated transport policies **58**.27-8
    in the London Borough of Enfield **58**.13-14

Volume numbers appear first (in bold) followed by page numbers; a change in volume number is preceded by a semi-colon.

Vol. 3   The Animal Rights Debate
Vol. 4   The Euthanasia Issue
Vol. 10 Sexually Transmitted Diseases
Vol. 11 Fertility Rights
Vol. 16 Our Ageing World
Vol. 19 Looking at Vegetarianism
Vol. 20 Population Growth
Vol. 22 Confronting Child Abuse
Vol. 23 Sexuality
Vol. 25 The Changing Workplace
Vol. 27 The Censorship Issue
Vol. 28 The Global Warming Debate
Vol. 29 Gambling
Vol. 31 The Impact of the Internet
Vol. 32 Coping with Stress
Vol. 33 The Tourism Issue
Vol. 35 The Education Crisis?
Vol. 39 Alcohol Abuse
Vol. 40 The Future of Marriage
Vol. 43 A Consumer Society

Vol. 44 Confronting Domestic Violence
Vol. 46 Child Labour
Vol. 54 The Energy Debate
Vol. 55 Globalisation
Vol. 56 The Wealth Divide
Vol. 57 Waste Pollution
Vol. 58 The Transport Issue
Vol. 59 Issues in Sport
Vol. 60 Confronting Cancer
Vol. 61 Fitness
Vol. 62 Drugs and the Law
Vol. 63 The Racism Debate
Vol. 64 The Gender Issue
Vol. 65 Human Rights
Vol. 66 Self-Esteem
Vol. 67 Parenting
Vol. 68 Coping with Depression
Vol. 69 The Media
Vol. 70 Adolescent Health
Vol. 71 Abortion

Vol. 72 Obesity and Eating Disorders
Vol. 73 Dealing with Bullies
Vol. 74 Money Matters
Vol. 75 Lone-Parent Families
Vol. 76 The Water Crisis
Vol. 77 Self-inflicted Violence
Vol. 78 Threatened Species
Vol. 79 Dealing with Homelessness
Vol. 80 The Cannabis Debate
Vol. 81 Alternative Therapies
Vol. 82 Protecting our Privacy
Vol. 83 Dealing with Crime
Vol. 84 Mental Wellbeing
Vol. 85 The Housing Crisis
Vol. 86 Smoking and your Health
Vol. 87 Genetic Modification
Vol. 88 Food and Nutrition
Vol. 89 Refugees
Vol. 90 Human and Animal Cloning
Vol. 91 Disability Issues

in Nottingham **58**.29
public attitudes to **58**.3, 7, 16
road haulage **58**.8-9, 38-9
road user hierarchies **58**.28
in rural areas **58**.9
standards for disabled use **91**.8, 10, 17, 25
trees
and GM crops **87**.20, 37
and recycling **57**.34
species under threat of extinction **78**.12

U

ultrasound scanning **71**.21
underachievement, and low self-esteem **66**.3, 39
unemployment
and age discrimination **16**.16, 17, 20, 25
and child labour **46**.3
and depression in children and young people **68**.5
and educational qualifications **35**.3
and gender **64**.3
and homelessness **79**.12
housing and environmental decline **85**.14
and older workers **16**.16, 17, 20, 25
and people in their 50s **16**.8
and poverty **56**.2, 4
and prisoners on remand **83**.26
and teenage parenthood **75**.4
unfair dismissal **25**.17
investigation of claims of, and privacy rights **82**.26, 27
lesbian and gay employees **23**.33, 40
universities
animal experiments by **3**.7
costs of a university education **74**.38
disappointing enrolments and cutbacks **35**.22-3
and drug use **62**.18
funding **35**.23-4; **74**.19-20
gender differences in performance **64**.8-9
part-time courses **35**.23
popularity of different **35**.7-8
in Scotland **35**.23-4
students and mental illness **84**.32-3
see also colleges; further education; students
urban areas
alcohol-related violence in town centres **39**.19
and the extinction of animals **78**.6
older people living in **16**.4
proportion of the population living in **85**.29-30
renewal **85**.26, 35
wasteland as wildlife sites **85**.16-17
urban growth
in the developing world **20**.9, 11, 17-20, 33
and global water shortages **76**.3, 5, 15
and population growth **20**.2, 3

V

vaccines
for farm livestock **19**.32

production **87**.18
vandalism
helping to prevent **83**.35
rates of **83**.2
and yob-culture Britain **83**.5, 6
young people's attitude to **83**.18
vegan diets **19**.1, 6, 12
alternatives to animal products **19**.12, 13
costs of **19**.14
drinks **19**.14
famous vegans **19**.12, 13
and nutrition **19**.12, 13-14
and protein **19**.13, 16
and teenagers **19**.13-14
vegetarian food **19**.1
characteristics of **19**.6
cooking **19**.2, 11
foreign **19**.2
fruitarian **19**.1
giving up **19**.23
health benefits of **19**.15, 20, 26, 33
and healthy eating **19**.7, 9, 20
iron-rich foods **19**.3, 8
lacto-ovo-vegetarian **19**.1, 6
lacto-vegetarian **19**.1
macrobiotic **19**.1
market value of **19**.21
meat substitutes **19**.2, 21-2
and nutrition **19**.3, 9
and protein **19**.9
pulses **19**.2
ready-made foods **19**.2
sauces and gravies **19**.2
semi or demi vegetarian **19**.1
vegan **19**.1, 6, 12
vegetarians **19**.1-40; **88**.18
and animal rights **3**.3
and animal welfare **19**.6, 26, 33
becoming a vegetarian **19**.11
defining **19**.2, 6
and dieting **72**.14
eating out **19**.2-3
and the environment **19**.6-7, 26, 27, 33
and foot-and-mouth disease **19**.22
and heart disease **19**.7, 8, 16, 19, 20
life insurance scheme for **19**.19
percentage of in the population **19**.1, 21
resistance from family and friends **19**.11
verbal abuse
attacks on teachers **73**.28
of children with learning disabilities **73**.12-13
and school bullying **73**.17
in the workplace **73**.36
victims of crime **83**.6
racially motivated crime **63**.4, 7, 14-15, 17
young people as **83**.7, 14
videos
BBFC classification of **27**.20
impact of video technology **27**.28
R18 videos **27**.24, 33-4
video games and compulsive gambling **29**.37

violence
    and advertising **69**.14
    alcohol-related **39**.3, 6, 15, 18, 19, 24
    anti-globalisation **55**.5
    attacks on gay people **23**.14, 17, 19
    as a cause of stress **68**.2
    censorship of **27**.1
    children as victims of **22**.14
    and children's rights **65**.1, 2, 5, 22
    and computer games **27**.17
    and low self-esteem **66**.3, 6, 20
    and mental illness **84**.4, 18
    and the physical punishment of children **22**.25-6
    racial **63**.4, 7, 13-14, 13-15
    on radio **69**.37
    on television
violent crime
    domestic violence **83**.6
    gun crime **83**.3, 4, 18
    rates of **83**.1
    sentences for **83**.3
    surge in reports of **83**.3
    and young people **83**.15
vitamins **88**.2, 5, 6, 8, 13
    in milk **19**.18
    and vegan diets **19**.12, 14
    and vegetarian diets **19**.9
    young people and vitamin intake **70**.26

W

wages
    childcare workers **25**.36
    and children working illegally **25**.20-1
    and consumer spending **43**.1
    and domestic child labour **46**.4
    and football production in India and Pakistan **46**.16
    and gender inequality **56**.15
    inequality of incomes **43**.4, 13
    low paid work **56**.2, 15
    minimum wage **25**.17; **43**.4; **56**.13, 18; **64**.22

    salaries of male managers **64**.15, 16, 22
    sick pay **25**.18
    for students **74**.37
    and women in the workforce **64**.11, 12, 13
    and young workers **25**.17, 18
war
    and child soldiers **46**.2, 10, 29, 30, 32
    and children's rights **65**.1-2, 5, 22
    and poverty in the developing world **56**.22
    warfare research and animal experiments **3**.8
waste management
    and biomass energy **54**.12
    car tyres **57**.7-8
    composting **57**.18, 19, 21, 22, 24-5
    electrical goods **57**.7
    energy from industrial and domestic waste **54**.11, 36
    fridges **57**.7, 14, 17
    incineration **57**.1-2, 3, 6, 15
    litter **57**.9-13
    nationwide systems of waste management **57**.20
    reducing waste **57**.5, 19-20
    and responsible tourism **33**.27, 28
    scrap cars **57**.7
    and water consumption **76**.1, 4, 19, 32, 36
    zero waste policies **57**.39
water conservation **76**.1, 3, 22, 37-9
water consumption
    bottled water **76**.23, 27
    and eco-systems **76**.2, 16-17, 19
    groundwater sources for drinking **76**.7, 9, 12
    and the importance of water quality **76**.9
    lack of access to clean water **76**.8, 9
    largest users of water **76**.36
    and population growth **76**.22, 29
    reasons for growth in **76**.3, 5, 8
    in selected countries **76**.7
    statistics **76**.7, 9
    and waste **76**.1, 4, 19, 32, 36
    water requirements per person per day **76**.6
    and water shortages **76**.21-2
water management
    and agriculture **76**.18

Volume numbers appear first (in bold) followed by page numbers; a change in volume number is preceded by a semi-colon.

Vol. 3   The Animal Rights Debate
Vol. 4   The Euthanasia Issue
Vol. 10 Sexually Transmitted Diseases
Vol. 11 Fertility Rights
Vol. 16 Our Ageing World
Vol. 19 Looking at Vegetarianism
Vol. 20 Population Growth
Vol. 22 Confronting Child Abuse
Vol. 23 Sexuality
Vol. 25 The Changing Workplace
Vol. 27 The Censorship Issue
Vol. 28 The Global Warming Debate
Vol. 29 Gambling
Vol. 31 The Impact of the Internet
Vol. 32 Coping with Stress
Vol. 33 The Tourism Issue
Vol. 35 The Education Crisis?
Vol. 39 Alcohol Abuse
Vol. 40 The Future of Marriage
Vol. 43 A Consumer Society

Vol. 44 Confronting Domestic Violence
Vol. 46 Child Labour
Vol. 54 The Energy Debate
Vol. 55 Globalisation
Vol. 56 The Wealth Divide
Vol. 57 Waste Pollution
Vol. 58 The Transport Issue
Vol. 59 Issues in Sport
Vol. 60 Confronting Cancer
Vol. 61 Fitness
Vol. 62 Drugs and the Law
Vol. 63 The Racism Debate
Vol. 64 The Gender Issue
Vol. 65 Human Rights
Vol. 66 Self-Esteem
Vol. 67 Parenting
Vol. 68 Coping with Depression
Vol. 69 The Media
Vol. 70 Adolescent Health
Vol. 71 Abortion

Vol. 72 Obesity and Eating Disorders
Vol. 73 Dealing with Bullies
Vol. 74 Money Matters
Vol. 75 Lone-Parent Families
Vol. 76 The Water Crisis
Vol. 77 Self-inflicted Violence
Vol. 78 Threatened Species
Vol. 79 Dealing with Homelessness
Vol. 80 The Cannabis Debate
Vol. 81 Alternative Therapies
Vol. 82 Protecting our Privacy
Vol. 83 Dealing with Crime
Vol. 84 Mental Wellbeing
Vol. 85 The Housing Crisis
Vol. 86 Smoking and your Health
Vol. 87 Genetic Modification
Vol. 88 Food and Nutrition
Vol. 89 Refugees
Vol. 90 Human and Animal Cloning
Vol. 91 Disability Issues

costs of **76.**33

dealing with the water crisis **76.**22, 26-8

government and planned policies of **76.**8-9, 17

and multinational water corporations **76.**29-30

pricing mechanisms **76.**22, 32

and privatisation **76.**22-3, 32

water power

tidal power **54.**1, 3, 8, 11, 13, 40

wave power **54.**1, 3, 8, 10, 11, 13, 27

water supplies **76.**15-17

and climate change **28.**7, 12, 26, 35

financing the provision of **76.**31-2

and food production **76.**3, 4, 7, 18

and livestock cultivation **19.**7

and multinational water corporations **76.**29-30

and planned water management policies **76.**8-9, 17

and population growth **20.**6, 9, 13-14, 22, 23, 24

projected worldwide water use **76.**35

and the shrinking of mountain glaciers **28.**19-20

statistics **76.**1, 2, 4, 6, 8, 19, 20

and water as a human right **76.**24-5, 32

and water pollution **76.**10-11, 15

and water shortages **76.**15-17, 19, 21-2

water usage by sector **76.**3

and water users **76.**36

wildlife

captive breeding **78.**22

conservation **88.**32, 34

crime **78.**19, 38-9

and global warming **28.**20, 23-4, 30, 35

hunting and the welfare of **3.**28

illegal trade in **78.**21-2

killing of **78.**2, 4-5, 5-6

and the law **78.**16-17, 38-9

and litter **57.**9, 13

and new house-building in the south-east **85.**33

overcollecting **78.**22

and population growth **20.**6, 8-9, 14, 21, 22

rare species **78.**28

and responsible tourism **33.**4, 27, 28, 29

and suffering **3.**4

trade in live animals **78.**20-1

vulnerable species **78.**28

and water abstraction **76.**34, 36

wild animals captured for research **3.**7

wills **74.**16

wind power **54.**3, 15, 37

women

in abusive relationships **44.**1, 3, 34

age of marriage **40.**1, 3, 5, 6, 13, 20

remarriages **40.**7

and AIDS/HIV

in Africa **10.**17, 33

and preventive education **10.**38

young women **10.**25, 32, 33

and alcohol

abuse **39.**5, 6, 24

alcohol-related violence **39.**19

consumption guidelines **39.**8, 9, 25, 40

effects of **39.**10

health benefits **39.**37

health risks **39.**5, 26, 27, 37

in pregnancy **39.**26, 28, 35-6

and the workplace **39.**21

in the armed forces **64.**29-32

Asian **56.**13

attitudes to race and racism **63.**8

Bill of Rights for **44.**4

and birth rates **67.**3, 6

and body image **72.**31

body measurements of British women **61.**16

and body-fat levels **61.**15

and cancer **60.**3, 4, 5, 27

cervical cancer **60.**5, 14, 16

lung cancer **60.**15

see also breast cancer

car drivers **58.**6

and censorship **27.**31-2

and changing family patterns **67.**5

and changing trends in family life **40.**3

and child abuse **22.**3, 4, 6, 10, 33

childless **20.**26; **40.**1

in China **20.**31

in cohabiting relationships with children **40.**9

and debt problems **43.**30-1, 38-9

decline in single older women **43.**2

and depression **68.**1, 4, 9

'baby blues' **68.**9, 14

post-natal **68.**9, 11, 12, 14-16, 25, 36

and stressful life events **68.**9

in developing countries **20.**2, 3, 9, 20; **55.**38

and dieting **72.**38

and divorce **40.**2

and domestic violence **44.**2-3, 24-5

earnings of black women **63.**19-20

effects of anabolic steroids on **59.**24

egg donation **11.**24

expenditure on toiletries **43.**2

and extra-marital affairs **40.**7

and extreme eating disorders **72.**24-5

and family planning **20.**25, 26, 27, 29-30

and fertility *see* fertility treatment; infertility

and football **59.**4, 11

and gambling **29.**3, 8

compulsive **29.**26

expenditure on **29.**9

and gender inequality **64.**1

and healthy eating **61.**30, 37; **72.**38

and homelessness **79.**10

and household financial management **64.**36

and Internet access **31.**1

iron deficiency in **19.**5

life expectancy **16.**6, 7, 29-30, 32, 33

managers, and bullying in the NHS **73.**33

maternal mortality **20.**25, 28, 29, 30, 36, 37, 39

and mental illness **84.**1

missing persons **79.**13

mother/child relationships **44.**31, 32

murdered by partners **44.**2-3, 8, 10, 22, 35

Muslim **63.**22

and obesity **61.**8, 12

and cancer **72.**9

and diabetes **72**.1, 8
and fat distribution **72**.7
rates of **72**.8, 10, 12
super-obese women **72**.6
waist size **61**.15
older women
centenarians **16**.9
and employment **16**.1, 3, 8, 13, 14
increase in retirement age **16**.26
inequalities of **16**.7
living alone **16**.2, 3
marital status **16**.2, 3
in the media **16**.12
numbers in the UK **16**.1, 3
oldest old **16**.4
proportion of the population **16**.9
and osteoporosis **61**.22, 26
and pelvic inflammatory disease (PID) **10**.1, 6, 7, 11
and physical activity **61**.2, 4, 11
and pornography **27**.1
and poverty
in the developing world **56**.22, 33
in the UK **56**.15
pregnant women **88**.7
pregnant women and cannabis **80**.15, 19
prisoners **83**.9
and pro-poor tourism **33**.34
rough sleepers **79**.10
and self-injury **77**.12-14
and sexually transmitted infections **10**.5, 9-10
chlamydia **10**.6, 9, 11
genital herpes **10**.8
getting help **10**.9-10
gonorrhoea **10**.6-7, 9
reducing risk of **10**.9, 10
single homeless **79**.19
and smoking **60**.27; **86**.1, 2, 5, 9, 14, 24, 25, 38, 154
and stalking **44**.12
and stress **32**.20, 30, 34-5
students **35**.7, 8-9, 35
and suicidal thoughts **77**.2
and suicide rates **77**.2

in their 50s **16**.8
trafficking of **46**.9, 19, 21-2
and university education **64**.8-9
and vegetarianism **19**.1
young women and cannabis **80**.2
young women leaving the parental home **67**.4
women in the workforce
earnings **64**.11, 12, 13, 15-16
and equal opportunities programmes **64**.24
equal pay *see* equal pay
and family responsibilities **64**.24, 26, 28, 33-4
and the 'glass ceiling' **64**.11, 12, 23
growth of **25**.1, 24
managers **25**.16, 30, 32; **64**.11, 12, 15-16, 23, 24, 39
and men **25**.31, 32-3
and occupation **64**.10, 11-12, 13, 19, 21, 25-6, 28
and part-time work **25**.1, 6, 7, 25; **64**.10, 11, 12, 13, 34-35
and the pay gap **64**.18-19, 24-5, 37
pregnant women **64**.34
and responsibility for household chores **25**.16
statistics **25**.25-6; **64**.16
and teleworking **25**.9
and travel patterns **64**.21
and the UK labour market **64**.13, 39
working from home **25**.6
working long hours **25**.6
young women in Europe **64**.10-11, 39
see also working mothers
work
child labour **65**.15, 16-17
and children's rights **65**.2, 5
and slavery **65**.34-5
and the Universal Declaration of Human Rights **65**.30
workplace
and cannabis users **80**.22
and disabled people **91**.15-16
dismissals
lack of confidence at work **66**.24
and mental health **84**.23
and privacy rights **82**.25-30
self-esteem as a workplace issue **66**.14

Volume numbers appear first (in bold) followed by page numbers; a change in volume number is preceded by a semi-colon.

Vol. 3   The Animal Rights Debate
Vol. 4   The Euthanasia Issue
Vol. 10   Sexually Transmitted Diseases
Vol. 11   Fertility Rights
Vol. 16   Our Ageing World
Vol. 19   Looking at Vegetarianism
Vol. 20   Population Growth
Vol. 22   Confronting Child Abuse
Vol. 23   Sexuality
Vol. 25   The Changing Workplace
Vol. 27   The Censorship Issue
Vol. 28   The Global Warming Debate
Vol. 29   Gambling
Vol. 31   The Impact of the Internet
Vol. 32   Coping with Stress
Vol. 33   The Tourism Issue
Vol. 35   The Education Crisis?
Vol. 39   Alcohol Abuse
Vol. 40   The Future of Marriage
Vol. 43   A Consumer Society

Vol. 44   Confronting Domestic Violence
Vol. 46   Child Labour
Vol. 54   The Energy Debate
Vol. 55   Globalisation
Vol. 56   The Wealth Divide
Vol. 57   Waste Pollution
Vol. 58   The Transport Issue
Vol. 59   Issues in Sport
Vol. 60   Confronting Cancer
Vol. 61   Fitness
Vol. 62   Drugs and the Law
Vol. 63   The Racism Debate
Vol. 64   The Gender Issue
Vol. 65   Human Rights
Vol. 66   Self-Esteem
Vol. 67   Parenting
Vol. 68   Coping with Depression
Vol. 69   The Media
Vol. 70   Adolescent Health
Vol. 71   Abortion

Vol. 72   Obesity and Eating Disorders
Vol. 73   Dealing with Bullies
Vol. 74   Money Matters
Vol. 75   Lone-Parent Families
Vol. 76   The Water Crisis
Vol. 77   Self-inflicted Violence
Vol. 78   Threatened Species
Vol. 79   Dealing with Homelessness
Vol. 80   The Cannabis Debate
Vol. 81   Alternative Therapies
Vol. 82   Protecting our Privacy
Vol. 83   Dealing with Crime
Vol. 84   Mental Wellbeing
Vol. 85   The Housing Crisis
Vol. 86   Smoking and your Health
Vol. 87   Genetic Modification
Vol. 88   Food and Nutrition
Vol. 89   Refugees
Vol. 90   Human and Animal Cloning
Vol. 91   Disability Issues

smoking **86.**17, 18, 19, 23, 25
workplace bullying **66.**24; **73.**25-39
workplace equality
   lesbian and gay employees **23.**32-5
worldwide poverty **56.**20-39
worthiness, and self-esteem **66.**21

X

X-linked inactivation **90.**37
xeno-transplantation **90.**30, 32-3, 35

Y

yoga **81.**3, 30, 39
young men *see* boys and young men; fathers
young offenders
   ethnic minority **63.**17
   and mental health problems **84.**1, 28-9
   see also crime and young people
young people
   affordable housing for **85.**3-4
   and AIDS/HIV **10.**23-5, 32-4
   and arranged marriages **40.**21, 22
   and cannabis **80.**3, 18
      attitudes to addictive drugs **80.**27
      and the cannabis economy **80.**8-9
      deaths **80.**16
      Government policies on **80.**25, 26
      home cultivation of **80.**33
      and the legalisation debate **80.**5
      and market saturation **80.**11
      and mental illness **80.**17
      under 18s and the police **80.**7, 25, 30, 31, 34
   cannabis users, and mental illness **68.**7
   and cohabiting relationships **40.**4, 6
   Connexions Service for **56.**18
   as consumers **43.**6-7
   and crime *see* crime and young people
   cruelty to animals by **3.**5
   and depression **68.**1, 4, 4-5, 8, 28-31
   in developing countries **20.**10-11, 33-4, 40
   and diet **70.**25-6
   disability rates **91.**4
   and domestic violence **44.**1, 3, 8, 27
   and drug abuse **39.**20, 24; **70.**6, 7, 8, 10, 14-16
      advice for teenagers **62.**12
      in Britain **62.**20
      cannabis **62.**31
      colleges and universities **62.**18
      employed young adults **62.**1-2
      in Europe **62.**7-8
      in schools **62.**4-5, 9
   and exercise **61.**1-4, 6-7, 10, 23-4, 26
   and film censorship **27.**1, 6
   and gambling **29.**2, 37-8; **43.**24
      compulsive gambling **29.**2, 19, 37-8
   and gay parents **67.**16
   going missing **79.**13-14

and healthy eating **88.**4
homelessness *see* homeless young people
and homosexuality **23.**5, 7, 8, 34
   images of **23.**13-14, 19
   prejudice among **23.**17-18
   and sex education **23.**10-12, 13-14
   and suicide **23.**19
house prices and first-time buyers **85.**6, 7
and identity (ID) cards, opposition to **82.**7
and iron deficiency **19.**5
marital breakups and the Internet **40.**36
and mental illness **84.**1, 5-6
   and education **84.**30-2
   in the family **84.**8-10
   schizophrenia **84.**13-15
   seeking help **84.**28
   symptoms of emotional and behavioural disorders **84.**30-1
and money matters **74.**1-4, 14-17
   attitudes to money **74.**2
   budgeting **74.**2, 3, 14-15, 23
   credit cards **74.**15, 16
   debt **74.**1, 2, 15, 16, 23-4
   and insurance **74.**2, 15
   paying bills **74.**2
   pension planning **74.**1-2
   savings **74.**15
   teenagers **74.**8-9
   tweenagers **74.**4
and parenting **67.**17, 18, 19, 20, 21, 24
and parenting classes **67.**23
parenting teenage children
   advice for parents **67.**17
   and effective parenting **67.**20, 21, 24
   and gay parents **67.**16
   and parental anxiety **67.**18
   and parental stress **67.**19
   and parenting classes **67.**23
   and stepfamilies **67.**13
and pensions **16.**27
and physical activity **70.**5
and pregnancy *see* teenage pregnancies
promoting emotional health and wellbeing **84.**24
as a proportion of the population **70.**3
and racial violence **63.**13
representation in the media **65.**3
and safer sex **10.**11
and self-esteem **66.**25-39
   and body image **66.**28, 31-2
   confidence and confidence building **66.**33
   getting help **66.**32
   improving **66.**26, 27-8
   and 'inner critics' **66.**27, 32
   political campaigning groups **66.**26
   unrealistic expectations **66.**27
and self-harm **70.**7, 36, 37-9; **77.**6-7, 9, 14
   prevention **77.**24-5, 27-9
   in schools **77.**30-1
and sex **10.**2
   sexual health **20.**33-4, 40
and sexual behaviour **70.**6, 7, 10-11, 13

sexual orientation **70**.6
and sexually transmitted infections **10**.5
rates of **10**.3
young women and chlamydia **10**.11
and shopping on the Internet **43**.23-4
and smoking **70**.4-10, 15, 17-19
and stepfamilies **67**.13
and stress *see* stress, and young people
and suicide **32**.8; **56**.3; **70**.1, 4, 6, 8, 36; **77**.1-2, 4-5, 17; **84**.1
and ChildLine counsellors **77**.5
effect on family and friends **77**.35, 36
prevention **77**.34-5
suicidal feelings **77**.1-2, 5, 31-2, 34-5
teenage smoking **86**.1, 2, 5-7
and transport costs **58**.15
unemployment rates **56**.2
and vegan diets **19**.13-14
and vegetarian diets **19**.1
views on asylum seekers **89**.17
views on marriage **40**.8, 16, 28
and violence on television **27**.35-6
and work *see* young workers
young men and HIV infection **10**.23-5
young people and alcohol **70**.6, 7, 16, 20-4
alcohol abuse **70**.7, 24
alcohol-related deaths **39**.6, 11, 24
binge drinking **39**.5, 18, 20; **70**.20, 21, 23, 24
consumption **39**.2-3, 7, 10, 13, 14, 24
and drug abuse **70**.15
in European Union countries **70**.9
health risks of **39**.15
and late-night bars **39**.19
and the law **39**.4; **62**.21
marketing to **39**.13, 14
measures to reduce the pressure to drink **39**.25
and parents **39**.13, 20
refusing to drink with friends **39**.33
in rural areas **39**.10
sales to underage teenagers **70**.22-3
and sexual behaviour **70**.10, 20
statistics **70**.21, 23-4

and suicide **70**.36
teetotallers **39**.40
under-age drinking **39**.6-7, 10, 12, 34
in Western European countries **39**.24-5
young workers **25**.17-23
apprentices **25**.19-20
employment rights for **25**.17
and health and safety at work **25**.18
and income tax **25**.18
managers **25**.22-3
and maternity benefits **25**.18
and National Insurance Contributions (NICs) **25**.18
protection against redundancy and dismissal **25**.17
schoolchildren working illegally **25**.20-1
and sick pay **25**.18
wages **25**.17
working time, rest breaks and holidays **25**.17
youth justice
binding over **83**.24
combination orders **83**.25
community sentences **83**.13, 16, 24-5, 30
and crime prevention **83**.33
and criminal responsibility **83**.29-30
custodial sentences **83**.24, 25, 30
detention of young offenders **83**.13
electronic monitoring **83**.25
exclusion orders **83**.25
and numbers of young offenders **83**.13
parenting orders **83**.30
and the police **83**.30
sentences and penalties **83**.24-5, 30
system **83**.30
young people in prison **83**.23
and Youth Inclusion Programmes (YIPs) **83**.20-2

Z

zero tolerance policies
and drug use in schools **62**.9
towards bullying and discrimination in the Army **73**.34
zygote **90**.5

Volume numbers appear first (in bold) followed by page numbers; a change in volume number is preceded by a semi-colon.

Vol. **3** The Animal Rights Debate
Vol. **4** The Euthanasia Issue
Vol. **10** Sexually Transmitted Diseases
Vol. **11** Fertility Rights
Vol. **16** Our Ageing World
Vol. **19** Looking at Vegetarianism
Vol. **20** Population Growth
Vol. **22** Confronting Child Abuse
Vol. **23** Sexuality
Vol. **25** The Changing Workplace
Vol. **27** The Censorship Issue
Vol. **28** The Global Warming Debate
Vol. **29** Gambling
Vol. **31** The Impact of the Internet
Vol. **32** Coping with Stress
Vol. **33** The Tourism Issue
Vol. **35** The Education Crisis?
Vol. **39** Alcohol Abuse
Vol. **40** The Future of Marriage
Vol. **43** A Consumer Society

Vol. **44** Confronting Domestic Violence
Vol. **46** Child Labour
Vol. **54** The Energy Debate
Vol. **55** Globalisation
Vol. **56** The Wealth Divide
Vol. **57** Waste Pollution
Vol. **58** The Transport Issue
Vol. **59** Issues in Sport
Vol. **60** Confronting Cancer
Vol. **61** Fitness
Vol. **62** Drugs and the Law
Vol. **63** The Racism Debate
Vol. **64** The Gender Issue
Vol. **65** Human Rights
Vol. **66** Self-Esteem
Vol. **67** Parenting
Vol. **68** Coping with Depression
Vol. **69** The Media
Vol. **70** Adolescent Health
Vol. **71** Abortion

Vol. **72** Obesity and Eating Disorders
Vol. **73** Dealing with Bullies
Vol. **74** Money Matters
Vol. **75** Lone-Parent Families
Vol. **76** The Water Crisis
Vol. **77** Self-inflicted Violence
Vol. **78** Threatened Species
Vol. **79** Dealing with Homelessness
Vol. **80** The Cannabis Debate
Vol. **81** Alternative Therapies
Vol. **82** Protecting our Privacy
Vol. **83** Dealing with Crime
Vol. **84** Mental Wellbeing
Vol. **85** The Housing Crisis
Vol. **86** Smoking and your Health
Vol. **87** Genetic Modification
Vol. **88** Food and Nutrition
Vol. **89** Refugees
Vol. **90** Human and Animal Cloning
Vol. **91** Disability Issues